BREAMISH & TILL:

FROM SOURCE TO TWEED

Also by Antony Chessell

The Life and Times of Abraham Hayward, Q.C., Victorian Essayist 'One of the two best read men in England', Lulu Publishing, 2009

A Small Share in the Conflict; The Wartime Diaries and Selected Correspondence of Flt Lt Henry Chessell (R.A.F. Intelligence Branch), Lulu Publishing, 2009, edited by Antony Chessell

The Short and Simple Annals of the Poor; Some Family Ramblings, Lulu Publishing, 2010, private circulation only

Coldstream Building Snippets   Cans, Quoins and Coursers, Lulu Publishing, 2010

The Braw Trees of Coldstream, Lulu Publishing, 2011

Avis M. Chessell, *The Sixpence That Grew and other Antony Trumpington Stories*, Lulu Publishing, 2011, private circulation only, edited by Antony Chessell

Leet Water From Source to Tweed, Lulu Publishing, 2012

BREAMISH & TILL:

FROM SOURCE TO TWEED

Antony Chessell

**Foreword by
Rt. Hon. Lord Joicey,
Ford & Etal Estates**

Published by TillVAS

First published in 2014

Till Valley Archaeological Society (TillVAS)

Northumberland www.tillvas.com

Antony Chessell asserts the moral right to be identified as the author of this work

A catalogue record for this book is available from the British Library

ISBN 978-1-291-58938-2

Typeset in Times New Roman

Printed and bound in Great Britain by *Lulu*

Front cover: River Till, looking south from Twizel road bridge

Cover design and photograph by the author

To the people of the Till and Breamish Valleys

Past, Present and Future

View of the lower reach of the R. Till, north from Twizel Bridge. Just visible is
the sandstone cliff below Twizel Castle, which is hidden behind the trees.

CONTENTS

ILLUSTRATIONS & ACCESS

The illustrations have not been listed in a separate table and they just appear within the text with explanatory captions. However, they are referenced in the index. Most photographs are from the author's collection and other illustrations and maps are from the stated sources. The author has taken note of Natural England's *The Countryside Code* during his travels (*see* Catalogue Code: NE326, accessible online at www.naturalengland.org.uk/publications). He has also complied with the law relating to rights of way and any readers travelling in his footsteps will want to do likewise. The legal position may be summarized as follows:-

Open Access Land

Under the Countryside and Rights of Way Act 2000, the public can walk freely on mapped areas of mountain, moor, heath, downland and registered common land without having to stick to paths, but with an emphasis on conservation of geology and wildlife.*

At all times of the year dogs must be kept on a short lead (no more than two metres) in the vicinity of livestock.

The Act allows a landowner or farmer to exclude or restrict access at their discretion in certain circumstances, e.g on grouse moors, but these powers have to be notified in advance to Natural England's Open Access Contact Centre in Bristol.

Public Rights of Way

All rights of way are legal highways and anyone can walk on them but some confer extra rights according to their type:-

Footpaths - open to walkers only, waymarked with a yellow arrow.

Bridleways – open to walkers, horse-riders and cyclists, waymarked with a blue arrow.

Restricted byways – open to walkers, cyclists, horse-riders and horse-drawn vehicles, marked with a plum-coloured arrow.

Byways open to all traffic – open to walkers, cyclists, horse riders, horse-drawn vehicles and motor vehicles, marked with a red arrow.

Local authorities and national park authorities must record the legal existence and location of rights of way on the definitive map, and ensure that they are open for public use. Landowners and occupiers must ensure that rights of way are not blocked by crops or other vegetation or otherwise obstructed, that the route is identifiable and the surface is restored soon after cultivation.

Permissive Paths

A permissive path is one used by permission of the landowner and not by right. Permission can be removed or suspended and the route or level of permitted use by foot, horse or vehicle may be changed at the wish of the landowner. There is no legal protection to users and no requirement on the landowner to maintain it.

Note: Much more information is available in publications by Natural England; they are accessible online and can be downloaded. Ordnance Survey maps from 2005 onwards show public rights of way; changes made since publication of maps should be well waymarked on the ground.

*Open access land is shown edged brown e.g. the upper Breamish Valley on OS 16.

FOREWORD

Rt. Hon. Lord Joicey, Ford & Etal Estates

Antony Chessell's portrait of the River Till is the latest in his series of studies of Borders topics. As he says, the river is the only English tributary of the Tweed, one of Scotland's great rivers. Despite its geography, the Till is governed by the River Tweed Commission, set up under an Act of Parliament established in 1857 and superceded at the time of Scottish devolution by the provisions of the Scotland Act 2008 (Tweed Act) Order 2006. The complexities which this entails are the stuff of legend, not least that an English river system is now effectively governed by the Scottish Parliament in Edinburgh.

It is apposite that this book should appear at a time when the relationship between England and Scotland is so much in focus, in the year of the independence referendum. We have just marked the 500th anniversary of the great Battle of Flodden, fought in 1513, in which the lower reaches of the Till played a major role in the strategy adopted by the English; and we will shortly be marking the 1000th anniversary of the Battle of Carham, fought in 1016 (or perhaps 1018). The latter marked the final end of the Kingdom of Northumbria and established the lower reaches of the Tweed as the border between England and Scotland. In the popular imagination, the border lands between these two countries have always been hazy, yet ironically the fixing of the River Tweed as the border at that time gives us one of the oldest border lines in Europe.

The twists and turns and meanders of the Till through the great Milfield Plain surely match the twists and turns in the history of this area. There are more to come perhaps, maybe as much scientific as political. The Till has long been famous for its large sea-trout which return from the sea in the spring, yet recent scientific work shows that the smaller sea-trout which run up the Till into the College Burn beneath The Cheviot in summer are genetically distinguishable, and also that most sea-trout are female. Despite the passage of the millennia we are scratching at the surface of some aspects of this fascinating river.

Antony Chessell's easy and approachable style, yet painstaking research, provides the opportunity for days of exploration in one of the loveliest and most interesting valleys of the Borderlands.

James Joicey, 2014

INTRODUCTION

In the foreword to a previous book, *Leet Water From Source to Tweed*, I reminisced on the reasons for my attraction to rivers, streams, lakes, ponds and waterfalls, citing childhood experiences on family holidays, adventures on 'jam jar and net' trips and camping with the Scouts. As an adult, mountaineering in North Wales, the Lake District and Scotland brought close contact with upland streams, burns, tarns, lakes, lochans and waterfalls, sometimes with the added thrills of freezing 'wild swimming' and even of 'skinny dipping'.

I am not alone in liking rivers, streams and the features associated with them—after all, the readers of this book are part of that company. There is so much to see and experience—the scenery, the animals, birds and insects, and the plants that grow beside and in the water. Also, in Britain there is so much history to discover, always within a short distance of water. Of course, many things have to be looked for, but searching and casting around rather than taking things at face value, will repay the 'effort' if that is what it is.

My first experience of Northumberland came from a walking holiday in 1960 when a friend and I stayed at a Holiday Fellowship Centre at Alnmouth. During those two weeks, we traversed a variety of scenery from the tors and moors of the Cheviots down through fields and woods past prehistoric settlements, taking in ancient roads and tracks, to the coast with its castles, cliffs, dunes and beaches.

We came across so many rivers and streams winding their way out of the hills and it was a revelation to discover such a beautiful, unspoilt and sparsely populated landscape that seemed to have everything and yet was completely unknown to many people in other parts of Britain.

Now, my wife and I are fortunate to live just across the Scottish border so that we are close enough to take advantage of all that Northumberland has to offer—we do get the best of both worlds as we tell our visitors. The dividing line between those two worlds is the River Tweed, the course of which is mostly in Scotland although the England/Scotland border runs down the median line of the river in its lower reaches before the Tweed finally runs into England and out to the North Sea at Berwick. These terminal details do not affect the classification of the Tweed as being a Scottish river and the fourth longest at 97 miles, with the second largest catchment area (after the River Tay) at about 1,500 square miles. The River Tweed has nine major tributaries and their catchments are all in Scotland except for the second largest, the River Till in Northumberland, most of which is in England. The upper part of the Till is called the River Breamish.

This book looks at the various sections of the River Breamish/Till between its source in the Cheviot hills down to its junction with the River Tweed at Tillmouth. It does not set out to be a comprehensive history of the area or a detailed guide to geology, flora and fauna and it is not a guide to archaeological sites and digs—it is a subjective journey and things only crop up on an 'as and when' and selective basis at the whim of the author. There is a wealth of literature out there for serious and not so serious students of archaeology, geology and flora and fauna. Information can be found in sources from the eighteenth century onwards, some of it listed in the Notes or as further reading on page 252.

The author hopes that readers will visit many of the places mentioned in the book, as the route is one of great variety and contrast with so much to see between source and mouth. It is not possible to walk the whole length of the rivers using public access (although it is for the upper reaches of the Breamish); some stretches can be walked whereas, for others, it is necessary to 'dip in and out' at points that are accessible to the public. This has been the author's method after taking the early decision not to walk on land that would require the permission of the landowner or occupier (except once). Nothing much is lost by doing so as there are plenty of public access points along the way. The 'armchair' approach, which formed part of the walker's preparation, is to follow the journey on the OS Explorer maps OL16, 332, 339 and 340 and other maps in the book.

For the walker, the advice is to take plenty of layered clothing to cope with the variable Northumberland weather. Good boots and windproof and waterproof outer layers, gloves and headgear are essential as well as map, compass, food, water and, a companion, as the upper part of the Breamish valley, in particular, is serious hill-walking country with snow, wind and rain to match. However, surprisingly often, sunhat and suncream are necessary and should not be left behind.

Antony Chessell, Coldstream, Scottish Borders, 2014

ACKNOWLEDGEMENTS

I wish to thank Lord Joicey of Ford & Etal Estates for kindly agreeing to write the Foreword. Apart from his strong family connection to the lands of the lower Till valley, James Joicey is a Director of Flodden 1513 Ecomuseum Ltd. and TillVAS is closely involved with the sites which are at the very heart of the museum.

I am grateful to my publishers for giving me a free rein to write a subjective account of the course of the two rivers. This means that all statements in the book are my responsibility and are not put forward as representing the views of TillVAS. Likewise, any errors are my own.

I particularly wish to thank Heather and John Pentland who kindly accompanied me to the source of the River Breamish, providing me with the best of company and also acting as a standby safety team in case I needed to be howked out of a cleugh.

I also wish to thank Lady Caroline Douglas-Home and Maureen Charlton for their support and for providing me with very useful information.

In addition, a special thank you to my wife, Gwen, who has carried out valuable proof-reading and who, as on previous occasions, has accompanied me on some expeditions, put up with my absences on others and encouraged me throughout.

Antony Chessell

1

Setting the Scene

The River Till in its upper reaches is known as the River Breamish, the one becoming the other at Bewick Mill, a point almost equidistant between Wooler and Alnwick as the crow flies. The change of name is recorded in an old rhyme:

The foot of Breamish and the head of Till,

Meet together at Bewick Mill. (Anon.)

Together, the two rivers have a length of, say, 50 miles (82 km.) but it is difficult to be precise because of the many twists and turns taken by both rivers. The Breamish/Till catchment is mainly in Northumberland but it spans the Scottish border towards the headwaters of the Bowmont Water. The main tributaries of the Breamish/Till are the Lilburn, Hetton Burn, Wooler Water and River Glen (called the Bowmont Water upstream from Westnewton). The River Till/Breamish, itself, is the only tributary of the Tweed to flow wholly within England.

Of the nine major tributaries of the Tweed, the Till has the second largest catchment area of 367 sq.miles (950 sq.km.).[1] As an English tributary, it is classed as a 'river', whereas the Scottish tributaries are all described as 'Waters' although the Teviot Water is also described as the River Teviot and is shown as such on Ordnance

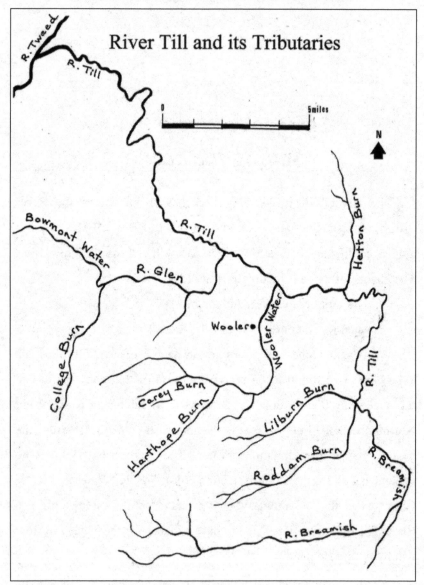

River Till and its Tributaries

Survey maps. The Till catchment forms part of the 1,930 sq.miles (5,000 sq.km.) River Tweed Catchment which, because of its diverse landscapes and rich variety of habitats and species, is designated as both a Site of Special Scientific Interest (SSSI) and a Special Area of

Conservation (SAC). The Till's meandering and often slow moving journey down to the faster moving Tweed was the cause of another local and unattributable rhyme:

> Tweed said to Till,
>
> "What gars ye rin sae still"
>
> Till said to Tweed,
>
> "Though ye rin wi speed
>
> And I rin slow
>
> Wha ye droon ae mon
>
> I droon twa!" (Anon.)

This aptly describes the deceptiveness of the R. Till whose calm character can change rapidly when the river is in spate. Its quicksands and unstable banks and ledges can be particularly dangerous, so much so that it is quite able to 'droon twa' to the Tweed's 'ae mon'.

It is one of the functions of the Environment Agency to assess the flood risk across England and Wales and to draw up Catchment Flood Management Plans (CFMPs). *The Till and Breamish CFMP* was published in 2009 and considers all types of inland flooding, from rivers, ground water, surface water and tidal flooding (the latter because the area extends to Berwick-upon-Tweed); it establishes flood risk management policies for the long term, taking into account the likely impact of climate change.[2] The Agency breaks down the risk of flooding into two parts: the chance (probability) of a particular flood and the impact (consequence) that the flood would have if it happened.

In the upper part of the Till and Breamish catchment area, the river can react quickly to rainfall during a flood event but levels tend to fall more quickly than in the lower, flatter parts of the catchment where flooding tends to last longer. Based on a one per cent probability of a flood in any one year, the Agency has estimated that there are 281 residential properties and 18 commercial properties at risk from a probability flood. Also at risk are four Scheduled Ancient Monuments (SAMs) and 0.23 kilometre squared, of registered parks and gardens at risk of flooding. There are 9.7 kilometre squared of SAC and SSSI at risk but, of this, 7.5 kilometre squared of this flooding has no detrimental impact and in some of the remaining sites flooding may even have a positive impact—this would be from the deposition of nutrients. Just over 51 kilometre squared of agricultural land is at risk during a one per cent probability flood. The comparatively few buildings at risk are concentrated in Wooler and smaller villages such as Norham, Powburn, Kirknewton and Akeld. The large areas of agricultural land at risk are in the Kirknewton, Wooler and Fenton areas.

The Environment Agency believes that climate change will produce more frequent and intense storms causing more widespread and regular flooding from drainage systems and rivers and there will be an increase in winter rainfall with an increased likelihood of large-scale floods. However, only an additional 26 properties have been identified as being at risk.

In view of these figures, the Environment Agency considers the risk of flooding to be low in the Till and Breamish CFMP due to the rural nature of the catchment; the history of flooding records a big flood in 1792 when two arches of the Wooler Bridge were swept away and the Great Borders Floods of 1948 when large areas of the catchment were flooded in Wooler, Powburn and Tweedmouth. Flooding has occurred since but not on such a scale. Major flooding occurred in 2008 and 2009; then, the R. Glen changed its course.

The 2008 flooding was severe enough to generate the *Cheviots Flood Impact Study*, commissioned by Cheviot Futures and funded by Northumberland National Park Authority, Scottish Borders Council, Northumberland Strategic Partnership, Environment Agency, Natural England and North East Climate Change Partnership.[3] The aim of the study was to capture the impact of the floods on the local population, by providing a record of events and examining the physical impacts and extent of the flooding in the Till catchment, gather personal experiences and impressions of those caught up in the floods, look at the socio-economic impacts on individuals and their livelihoods and provide a preliminary estimate of the economic impact of the flooding on the rural community. The study also aimed to assess the existing mechanisms in place to deal with flooding and make recommendations for improvements.

The work of the Environment Agency and other bodies, aided by such studies and by measurement of river levels and flow rates, aims to minimize the deleterious effects of flooding in the catchment area and to plan how best to deal with possible future threats. River levels and flow rates are monitored by the Environment Agency at River Level Stations. Data is recorded electronically at these monitoring stations by sensors in the river every 15 minutes and sent back to the Agency via telemetry systems to their databases. River levels are measured in metres related to a specific datum and river flows are measured in cubic metres per second. There are monitoring stations at Heaton Mill on the R. Till and at Coldgate Mill and Wooler, both of these being on the Wooler Water. The information is published online to help the Environment Agency fulfil its statutory duty because it recognizes that the up to date information may be helpful to others.[4]

The course of the Rivers Breamish and Till can be traced (in order from source to mouth) on OS Explorer maps OL16, 332, 340 and 339 at 4 cm. to 1 km. ($2^1/_2$ inches to 1 mile). The upper reaches of the R. Breamish are characterized by steep-sided valleys with narrow flood-plains as the river falls down from the Cheviot massif. At Ingram, the valley becomes wider with terraces of glacial drifts on either side as far as Powburn. Downstream from here, the river channel, terraces and flood plain have been affected by sand and gravel extraction which is still being carried on at a 33 hectares site at Low Hedgeley, east of the A697 road, producing 70,000 tonnes per annum as reported in 2009/2010.[5]

Beyond this, the Breamish and then the Till meander through an alluvial valley floor flanked by undulating glacial and glaciofluval drift with a Fell Sandstone escarpment to the east. West and north-west of Weetwood Bridge, near Wooler, the Till valley opens out into the Milfield Plain; the river meanders across the plain within flood embankments until, north of the village of Milfield, the valley gradually narrows between terraces. Below Etal, the river flows in a narrow gorge as far its junction with the R. Tweed at Tillmouth. Both rivers flow through a landscape that has been determined by its geology, by glacial action, by weather and by human activity.

SETTING THE SCENE

The Till and Breamish valleys lie within ancient geological formations. The England/Scotland border is roughly on the line of the Iapetus Suture, the result of the junction between two continents originally separated by the Iapetus Ocean. Plate tectonic movements caused the continents to close the ocean and come together in a series of collisions in an event known as the Caledonian Orogeny. This was between 490 and 420 million years ago.

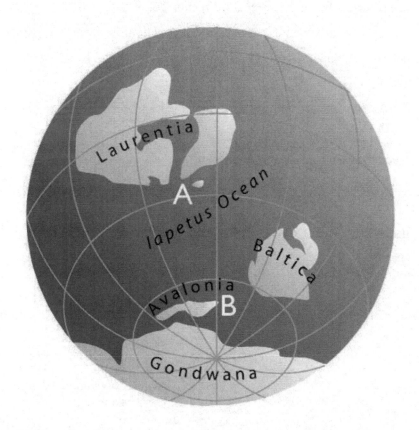

Globe showing position of the Iapetus Ocean, approximately 500 million years ago and the areas that became the present-day Great Britain and Ireland.
A – Scotland and the north of Ireland; B - England, Wales and southern Ireland.
Reproduced in black and white from original coloured diagram by permission of the British Geological Survey © NERC. All rights reserved. CP12/131.

Originally, the continents of Laurentia, Baltica and Avalonia were in the southern hemisphere with Avalonia, (which then included England, Wales, parts of mainland Europe and parts of the maritime states of North America) at a latitude of about 60° south. The collision of continents formed the Caledonian mountain belt and, eventually, the land masses moved into the northern hemisphere and separated into their present day formations. The Iapetus Suture has been buried by more recent sediments but the British Geological Survey can still identify its shallow inclination northwards beneath northern England from geophysical imagery data. These ancient events together with subsequent movements and deposition of material have determined the geological history of the area.[6]

The timeline of geological events since the closure of the Iapetus Ocean is divided into Eras and Periods as shown below.[7]

Era	Time (millions of years ago)	Period	Event
Palaeozoic	443	Silurian	mud/sand laid down in Iapetus Ocean. Iapetus Ocean closed.
	417	Devonian	first mountains built (Cal. Orogeny). Cheviot volcano & granite intrusion mountains eroded to sea level.
	354	Carboniferous	extension & subsidence of earth's crust. shallow seas, deltas and coal swamps. Whin sills intruded.

Era	Time	Period	Event (cont.)
	290	Permian	formation of mineral veins. uplift & erosion upland deserts, meandering rivers
Mesozoic	248	Triassic	and adjacent evaporating shallow seas to west & east.
	205	Jurassic	
	142	Cretaceous	
Cenozoic (Cainozoic)	65	Palaeogene	opening of the North Atlantic begins & basalt dykes intruded from Hebridean volcanos. uplift
	24	Neogene	erosion by rivers, rain & wind
	2	Quaternary	glaciers, meltwater & frost action sculpt the present day
	0		landscape.

The British Geological Survey has put the great length of the geological timeline into perspective by representing the whole of earth history by a single day. In the above extract, the oldest, Silurian rocks would have been formed around 9.45 pm, the Carboniferous limestone between 10.10 and 10.30 pm and the Quaternary ice ages would have begun at less than one minute to midnight. Man first walked across this landscape at less than one second to midnight.

The following map and key show the underlying geological structure of Northumberland; the Rivers Breamish and Till flow east through the Devonian volcanic Cheviot formations marked B and N and then northwards through Carboniferous formations C, D and E.[8]

9

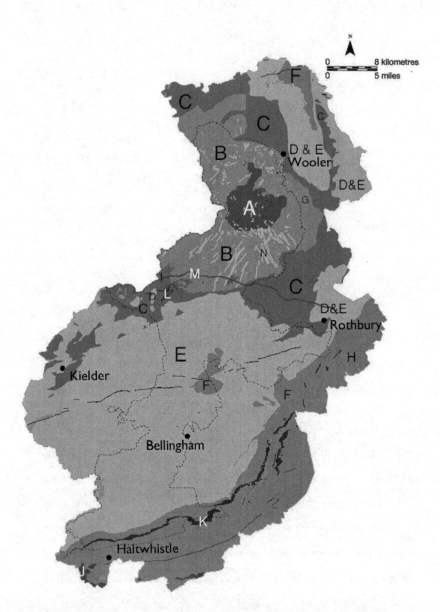

Simplified geological map of part of Northumberland with a key on the following page. Reproduced in black and white from original coloured map and key with author's overlaid letters, all by permission of the British Geological Survey © NERC. All rights reserved. CP12/131.

SETTING THE SCENE

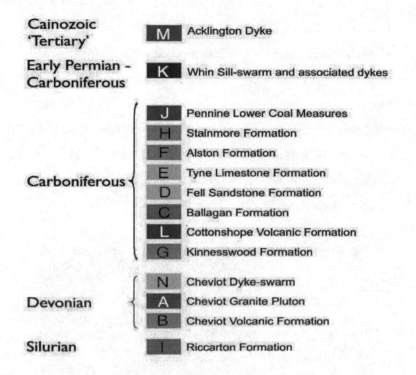

Cainozoic 'Tertiary'
- **M** Acklington Dyke

Early Permian – Carboniferous
- **K** Whin Sill-swarm and associated dykes

Carboniferous
- **J** Pennine Lower Coal Measures
- **H** Stainmore Formation
- **F** Alston Formation
- **E** Tyne Limestone Formation
- **D** Fell Sandstone Formation
- **C** Ballagan Formation
- **L** Cottonshope Volcanic Formation
- **G** Kinnesswood Formation

Devonian
- **N** Cheviot Dyke-swarm
- **A** Cheviot Granite Pluton
- **B** Cheviot Volcanic Formation

Silurian
- **I** Riccarton Formation

The map shows the underlying bedrocks formed during the geological eras and periods from 443 million years ago. The oldest rocks of the upper Breamish valley are the volcanic rocks belonging to the Cheviot formation from the Devonian period; these are igneous rocks formed from andesitic lava or magma into which were intruded granites of the central Cheviot Granite Pluton (from Pluto, the classical god of the underworld) and the radiating dykes of the Cheviot Dyke-swarm, many of which are reddish in colour when weathered, compared with the grey or blue of the volcanic rocks.

The underlying bedrock for the lower Breamish valley and the valley of the Till is from the Carboniferous period when limestones and sandstones were laid down in shallow seas and

11

lagoons. There are the mudstones, siltstones and cementstones of the Ballagan Formation, so named after Ballagan Glen north of Glasgow because the same sequence continues into Northumberland. The Ballagan formation rocks are relatively soft and easily eroded by weathering and subsequent glacial action. The other sedimentary formations are the Tyne Limestone Formation, which tends to lie below other formations and contains coal seams and the Fell Sandstone Formation which, on exposure as rocky outcrops and crags, is a friable, medium-grained sandstone.

Goats Crag, east of the village of Ford. A Fell Sandstone outcrop to the east of the Milfield Plain—a good lunch stop for a TillVAS expedition.

However, since then, these formations have been overlaid in many places by material from Quaternary deposits. During this time, successive glaciers covered the whole of northern Europe probably down as far as the R. Thames and glacial flow carved out 'U'- shaped valleys, eroded mountains and deposited rocks, sand and gravel along the direction of travel. Material visible today is probably left over from the end of the last Ice Age, about 11,000 years ago.[9]

In north Northumberland, it seems that the Cheviot massif deflected the west to east glacial flow around it on the north and south sides. To the north of The Cheviot and across the Tweed valley, the Tweed ice flow left material in large and small linear deposits, drumlins, megadrumlins and megaflutes, all aligned in a west/east or south-west/north-east direction. They are a characteristic feature in the landscape, recognized by the switchback roads across the wide Tweed valley. To the east of the Cheviot massif, the deposits are glaciofluvial meaning that material was left by glacial meltwater. In the Till valley between Wooler and Powburn, there are mounds and hummocks of sand and gravel dissected by channels formed by the meltwater.

Also to the east of the Cheviot massif there is evidence of ancient lake deposits in the form of soft, red clays across the Milfield Plain although they are hidden by topsoil and muds. The lake is thought to be an ice-dammed lake situated at the margin of the retreating Tweed basin ice sheet; it is overlain on the west side by fan deposits from the R. Glen, a tributary of the R. Till and the ice dam probably caused a diversion of the course of the river in its lower reaches.[10] Apart from the underlying bedrock and original glacial deposits, there are substantial alluvial deposits in the Breamish and Till valleys caused by the rivers and their tributaries carving through the glaciofluvial material, mixing it up and spreading it out to form fertile floodplains and terraces.[11]

In the Till Valley, the Fell Sandstone formation consists of underground layers of permeable rock from which groundwater can be extracted. This is the only major acquifer in the Till Valley as defined by the Environment Agency in its 2008 *Till Catchment Abstraction Management Strategy* (CAMS).[12] Since 2010, major acquifers have mostly been redefined as Principal Acquifers to coincide with their definition in the EU Water Framework Directive and to reflect their ability to provide a high level of water storage which may support a water supply and/or a river base flow on a strategic scale. In the Till CAMS, the Fell Sandstone, as a 'Principal Acquifer', is the only major source for groundwater abstraction for drinking water and there are no licensed surface water abstractions except that water is abstracted from the rivers for agricultural use such as for crop spraying. There are other 'Secondary Acquifers' enabling groundwater abstraction from other rock formations. In 2008, there were five licences authorizing groundwater abstraction and one for industrial and commercial purposes.

The Till CAMS is about 700 sq.km. and covers the Rivers Till, Glen, Breamish and Wooler Water and includes the towns of Berwick-upon-Tweed and Wooler. The catchment is divided into areas that can be managed by the Environment Agency as individual units of which there are two types; the first covers management units which are surface water only or a combination of surface water and associated groundwater; the second (only one in 2008) covers groundwater only—the important Fell Sandstone area.

The management units enable the Environment Agency to

monitor the quality of the abstracted water and to publish groundwater quality reviews such as that set out in the most recent and very detailed *Till and Northumberland Rivers Fell Sandstone Review*[13] which examines the geography, geology, hydrogeology, several 'pressures and drivers' and groundwater quality including inorganic and organic chemical constituents. Reassuringly, the groundwater quality is described in summarized terms as 'generally reported to be good' with the water being 'typically of a calcium magnesium bicarbonate type although several results are enriched with chloride or sulphate'. Elevated concentrations of nitrates have been found in the northern part of the monitoring unit (the lower reaches of the Till valley and east towards Berwick) due to arable farming and managed grassland.

As to the quality of river water rather than groundwater, samples taken from the Till catchment score very highly on the indices prepared by the Environment Agency, making it one of the cleanest rivers in England and Wales. The Northumberland National Park Authority is able to claim that 'According to the Environment Agency's 2009 assessment of waterways, four out of five cleanest rivers in Britain are sourced in Northumberland National Park'.[14] Two of the four are the R. Breamish and the Linhope Burn which is a tributary of the R. Breamish. The Park attributes the pure water to the type of farming that has conserved the moorland character of the area and to its low population. These high rivers and burns fall from the Cheviot Hills, a landscape that the Park claims to be 'officially the most tranquil in the country'.[15]

The Environment Agency takes around 7,000 samples at

regular intervals from rivers and canals throughout England and Wales and analyses their chemistry, biology, nitrate and phosphate content. They are collected twelve times a year except for biology, samples which are collected every three years. Chemistry and biology are graded from A to F (very good to bad) and nitrates and phosphates are graded 1 to 6 (very low levels to very high levels). Samples were taken in 2009 from the College Burn, R. Glen, Harthope Burn, Wooler Water, Hetton Burn, Lilburn Burn, Roddam Burn and the Till itself at the confluence with the Tweed.[16] The results for chemistry and biology are consistently graded A; nitrates and phosphates are often graded 1 but some sites produce levels from 2 to 4.

The classification system used by the Environment Agency for twenty years is to become more rigorous in future years, as the new system will be looking at over 30 measures in order to implement the requirements of the European Water Framework Directive. This was adopted and came into force in 2000 but contained implementation deadlines to be complied with by member nations up to 2015. The Directive was transposed into UK law in 2003 by an Act of Parliament for Scotland and by way of a Statutory Instrument for England and Wales.

The good quality of water in the Till catchment, particularly in the higher reaches of the Breamish, as in the photograph on the next page and in the tributaries flowing down from the Cheviot Hills, means that the water courses are home to migrating salmon and sea trout, to otters, dippers and other animal, bird and plant life that can flourish in such a pure environment.

As to the origin of 'Breamish', Eneas Mackenzie, in 1825,

drawing on Jamieson, suggests that this may be from the Gaelic [more properly Celtic] *breme* meaning furious, raging, swelling and *uishg* or *uisge* meaning water. However, Henry Maclauchlan, in 1864, preferred *Brea-an-uisg*, the 'hill waters'.[17]

The water in the upper River Breamish is pure, clear, fast and noisy, even here at a comparatively low autumn level, as it tumbles over and around boulders and swirls around pools in the river-bed.

2

Breamish Head to Ingram Bridge

There is no doubt about the location of the source of the R. Breamish as it is clearly shown and named on the Ordnance Survey Explorer Map OL16. The Grid Ref. is NT90281820.

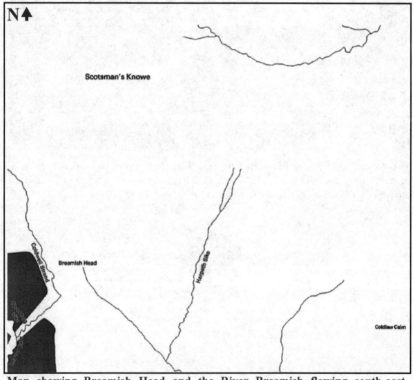

Map showing Breamish Head and the River Breamish flowing south-east. contains Ordnance Survey data © Crown copyright and database right 2014.

BREAMISH HEAD TO INGRAM BRIDGE

Breamish Head is situated between the 490 m. and 500 m. contour lines on a col, half a mile below, and south-south-west of, the mound of Scotsman's Knowe (650 m.) which is on the slopes of Cairn Hill (777 m.). Cairn Hill is on the ridge leading up to The Cheviot (815 m.) (neither are shown here—see OS map OL16) and there is a side branch of the Pennine Way leading over these two summits. To get an idea of scale, Scotsman's Knowe is a mile south-west of the summit of The Cheviot and the distance between Breamish Head and Coldlaw Cairn on the above map is less than three-quarters of a mile, as the crow flies.

The source of the Breamish can be located after a walk of six miles up the valley from the end of the road at Hartside along the surfaced and unsurfaced tracks up to and beyond High Bleakhope. The final section involves a trackless route across grassland and several watercourse ravines known as sikes, cleughs or strands. This is a wild and remote place, characteristics that apply to the whole of the upper Breamish valley; nevertheless, there is evidence of human activity even in this quite bleak landscape because of the fences that are present and the old boundary stones that stand alongside the fence that leads south to Bloodybush Edge. Original natural landscape has been grazed away by sheep and goats leaving grass and blanket bog with heather moorland on the surrounding hills. Also, close to the source of the Breamish is the start of a large forestry plantation that extends to the south-west.

Bleakness was not uppermost in the minds of my two companions and I on a warm, sunny morning in June as we were treated to vivid colours, the sparkling Breamish and a variety of

19

accompanying birdlife including curlews, oyster-catchers and sandpipers. The sky clouded over as we reached our objective but we had experienced a perfect approach all the way to the source; the timing was just right for lunch and the sandwiches tasted really good.

The point where the Breamish emerges from the ground is quite clear both visually and aurally even in summer when the grasses are high and might obscure the source. The infant river flows from a marshy collecting ground and immediately forms a definite, narrow channel of running water that chuckles and gurgles from its inception before passing under a boundary fence and quickly establishing its own small ravine. It may be said that the river starts as it means to go on, developing the liveliness that it maintains throughout its journey, a character that is transferred to the R. Till lower down until, finally, the combined waters meet the Tweed.

The col at Breamish Head is a narrow watershed between some of the many headwaters of the R. Coquet and the southernmost headwaters of the R. Till catchment; however, because of the proximity of the forestry plantation, the division between the two catchment areas is obscured by the trees to the west. The Caldwell Strand, seen on the map above, is one of a number of streams and burns draining south-west below the ridge of the Cheviot Hills before they combine and swing south and south-east to form the Rowhope Burn which joins the R. Coquet. The R. Breamish, on the other hand, flows south-east and is joined one quarter of a mile or so downstream by its first small tributary, the Harpath Sike. The burn flowing roughly east and then north-east of Scotsman's Knowe is the Harthope Burn which joins the Wooler Water (see also map on p. 2).

20

The source at Breamish Head. The stick shows the point at which the Breamish emerges from a marshy area and flows south-south-east in a narrow channel (in summer it is obscured by grass but can just about be made out here) towards and under the fence before turning south-east.

The col would have been a crossing point for travellers dropping down to the Till from the ridgeway now traversed by the Pennine Way or for those coming over from the Bowmont Water side. It must have witnessed the passage of many lawless bands of Scots and English cut-throats, cattle-thieves, kidnappers and plunderers during the unsettled times of the Border Reivers, say from the 13th century to the 17th century. Even if large armies kept to the main valleys and coastal routes, there must have been small raiding parties crossing here during the many English and Scots skirmishes and this, as well as the activities of the Reivers is probably reflected in some of

21

the place-names.

Allen Mawer has given a possible explanation for 'Harpath' as 'path of the army' from Old English *heriges-pæð*.[1] 'Sike' is a Scots and northern English term for a ditch or small stream that does not always contain running water. If the derivation of 'Harpath' is not certain, 'Scotsman's Knowe' (*knowe* meaning 'hillock') is a clear reference to some episode in cross-border raids or skirmishes. There is the 'Hanging Stone' (see note [2] for information) on Cairn Hill and just over a mile south-west of Breamish Head is 'Murder Cleugh' (*cleugh* meaning 'gorge', perhaps from Scots or Old English *clough*). Also, between two miles and three miles to the south is the prominent hill, 'Bloodybush Edge'; all are suggestive of violence and tragedy.[2]

The heather moorland is conserved as a habitat for grouse so even this upland area is only a semi-natural landscape. The highest grassy slopes have been described as the 'white lands' due to their bleached or frosted appearance, a description that, to me, conjures up an image of the Tibetan 'forbidden lands' of mystery and legend. Higher up the slopes, the heather moorland is home to the Mountain bumblebee, *Bombus monticola,* a small bumblebee sometimes known as the Bilberry bumblebee that has an orange abdomen and two lemon stripes on its thorax. It is also worth looking out for the spectacular Emperor moth, *Saturnia pavonia*; the female is larger than the male and has eye-like spots on its grey wings whereas the male is smaller with browner front wings and orange hind wings. Sometimes it is possible to spot a merlin and, on the edges of moorland, a curlew, which is the emblem of the Northumberland National Park.

Boggy areas contain carbon-storing peat and are carpeted by

Sphagnum moss, *Sphagnum*, that retains water, so preventing downstream flooding. The attractive pink heath plant, Bog rosemary, *Andromeda polifolia*, is a relative of heather that thrives in the moist acid soil along with the carnivorous Greater or English sundew, *Drosera anglica* and another member of the heather family, the edible Bog cranberry, *Vaccinium oxycoccos*.

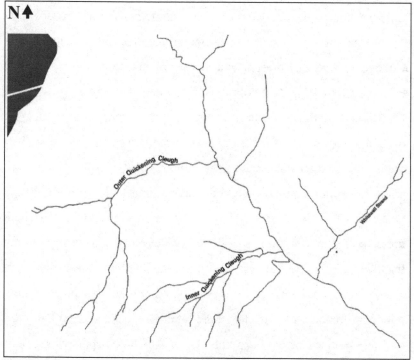

Continuation of previous map showing the R. Breamish flowing south-east with tributaries entering from west and east. The distance between Outer Quickening Cleugh and Inner Quickening Cleugh is under half a mile. Contains Ordnance Survey data © Crown copyright and database right 2014.

Another delicious treat for the high-level walker is the profuse blue bilberry, *Vaccinium myrtillus*, perhaps eaten whilst gazing across waving fields of Cotton-grass, *Eriphorum angustifolium,* which is a sedge rather than a grass and sometimes known as 'Scotsman's heid'. Cotton-grass with its distinctive white fluffy head is a good indicator of wet ground.

An animal living wild up here is the feral goat. The population in Britain has declined since primitive goats escaped or were turned out on to the hills some 150 years ago. The total population of primitive goats found wild in Scotland and the North of England may only be about 1,500 including family groups that survive in the Cheviot Hills, particularly above and down into the College Valley. The present goat-herds are said to be descendants of the breed first kept by Neolithic farmers and then by Anglo-Saxon, Danish and Medieval farmers up until the late eighteenth century. At that time, larger breeds were imported from abroad in order to satisfy the need for larger goats with short, smooth coats that provided more milk. The small, hairy British goat was no longer of use but, until the 18th and 19th century introduction of foreign goats, the old British breed was the only one in existence here. Larger groups come together during the rutting season in the autumn when there are clashes between the males. However, it is a matriarchal society with a dominant female as the leader of the herd. Females kid from February onwards with the newly born kids lying in sheltered spots whilst their mothers go off to graze before returning to them.[3]

Compared with Breamish Head, a more prominent east/west and west/east route across the ridge of the Cheviot Hills and one that would have seen more use, is the 'Salter's Road'. This is a track that crosses the col on the north side of Bloodybush Edge, dropping down across the southern slope of Nagshead Knowe into the Breamish

Valley where the two riverbanks are first shown on the map on p. 25. Salter's Road, having entered the Breamish Valley above High Bleakhope, leaves the valley again at Low Bleakhope from where it travels south-east over the moors and down to what is now the site of the medieval village of Alnham. Salter's Road is also known locally

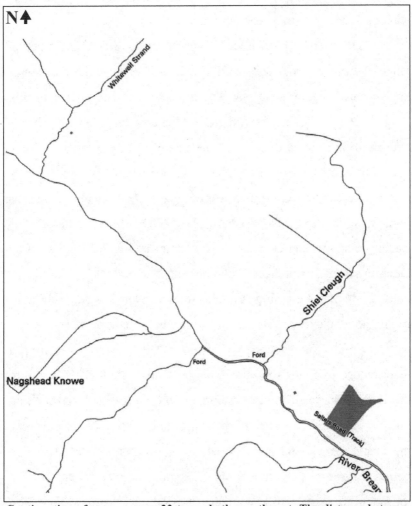

Continuation of map on page 23 towards the south-east. The distance between Whitewell Strand and Shiel Cleugh is about half a mile. Note Salter's Road. Contains Ordnance Survey data © Crown copyright and database right 2014.

as the 'Thieves' Road', a reference, no doubt to its Border Reiving past but became known as the 'Salter's Road' because of its use for carrying salt across from the coast into Scotland. Eneas Mackenzie stated that there were 153 salt pans at Howden Pans, Jarrow and North and South Shields in 1605 but that by 1825 when he was writing, there was little being done and, such panning as there was, was confined to North and South Shields.[4]

Three other historic cross-border tracks across the Cheviot Hills are further to the south-west. The ancient 'Clennell Street', once known as 'Ernspeth' from the Anglo-Saxon, *ern* and *pæth* meaning 'Eagle's Path', runs north-west from Alwinton and eventually heads over the Border towards Kelso. 'The Street' is another ancient drove road into Scotland from the upper R. Coquet (and its illicit whisky stills) but the most well-known is the Roman 'Dere Street' which runs north-west through what are now the MOD artillery ranges.[5] The routes are shown and described in two maps and guides published by Otterburn Ranges and the Northumberland National Park.[6]

The first two things to notice downstream from the source is, firstly, how quickly the Breamish forms a definite channel and even a gorge or ravine and, secondly, how soon it increases in size from a mere tendril to a small river with a substantial width. This is due to the large volume of water coming off the steep-sided surrounding hills within a short distance of the source and carving its way through the Cheviot rock and soil formations laid down in the Devonian period. In summer, the higher sikes, strands and cleughs are dry but the upper Breamish still maintains a good flow, although nothing compared with the torrents produced at other times of the year.

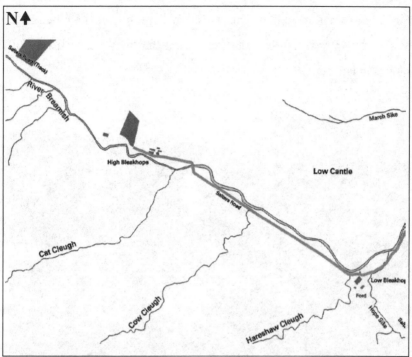

Continuation of map on p.25 showing the R. Breamish and Salter's Road past High Bleakhope as far as Low Bleakhope. The distance between the two farms is about half a mile. Contains Ordnance Survey data © Crown copyright and database right 2014.

The first stretch of the river down to the fords and the track's first junction with Salter's Road shown on p. 25 is through high moorland, dotted with occasional sheepfolds. Downstream from here, more sheepfolds are sited near two fords; there is a footbridge and an old, railway goods carriage is used as a fodder store. The valley bottom widens with small fields and meadows associated with the first human habitation at High Bleakhope farm and the ravines carved out by the infant Breamish and its short tributaries such as Cat Cleugh and Cow Cleugh, become more dramatic. My companions and I were surprised to see great swathes of bluebells so high up the valley at the top of the small woodland area at High Bleakhope. Their height at 300 m. to 350 m. (about 1,000 ft.) meant that they were still in full bloom in late June.

The R. Breamish just above High Bleakhope Farm. The ravine of Black Cleugh can be seen descending from the top right in the photo.

The whole of the Breamish valley down to Ingram is owned by Northumberland Estates (The Duke of Northumberland) or by the Percy family (Linhope Estate) and most of it also lies within the Northumberland National Park. This is the most northerly of the ten National Parks in England and covers over 1,030 sq.km (398 sq.miles). It was designated in 1956 and, like all the National Parks and also other areas defined as Areas of Outstanding Natural Beauty, is a 'Protected Area' whose aims and purposes are laid down in law.

28

The originating Act was the National Parks and Access to the Countryside Act 1949 but the original legislation was amended by The Environment Act 1995 which set out two statutory purposes:

1. Conserve and enhance the natural beauty, wildlife and cultural heritage, and

2. Promote opportunities for the understanding and enjoyment of the special qualities of National Parks by the Public.

National Park Authorities also have a duty to seek to foster the economic and social wellbeing of local communities within the National Parks. Each of the National Parks has its own special qualities that led to its designation, but they all relate to landscape and views, geology and geography, biodiversity and rare species and the archaeology and history of the area. Although the use and development of land is subject to statutory controls, the ethos of a National Park is a positive one by encouraging visitors and residents to benefit from nature and the environment, without destroying it.

Under 2. above, the National Park Authorities promote a wide range of visitor facilities but always have to seek the right balance between recreation and conservation. If there is any conflict between the two, the Authorities must have regard to the 'Sandford Principle' (named after the chairman of the National Parks Policy Review Committee in 1974) which states that 'Where irreconcilable conflicts exist between conservation and public enjoyment, then conservation interest should take priority'.[7]

The buildings at the tenanted High Bleakhope Farm, which must be one of the most remote farms in Northumberland, are the first buildings to be encountered below Breamish Head. Bleak it may be,

29

but Alan Mawer gives a possible derivation from the Old English *blæc* meaning 'black' or, confusingly, from the Middle English, *blāke*, or OE, *blāc*, meaning 'pale'. He doesn't make it any easier by suggesting that 'bleak' may be a Scandinavian form of OE *blāc*. 'Hope' is a Scottish and North-East England term from the OE *hop* meaning 'a small enclosed valley, especially a smaller opening branching out from the main dale, the upland part of a mountain valley, a blind valley'.[8]

High Bleakhope Farm looking upstream from the bridge taking Salter's Road across the R. Breamish (see map on p. 27).

This is sheep country because these upland areas are unsuitable for cultivation. There are enclosed grass meadows below High Bleakhope and these were covered in wild flowers when we were there in June. The endemic breed is the Cheviot sheep that was

30

recognized as a breed as early as 1372. Cheviots survive well in bleak, high, windswept conditions as they have a strong constitution. They also give easy lambing, mature fast and have a well-developed mothering instinct. The ewe has fine, hard white hair on her face, over her crown and on her legs. The rams can have horns. Cheviots are bred for their meat and, to a lesser extent, for their wool.[9]

However, perhaps most of the sheep to be seen up here are the Blackface sheep, the most numerous breed in the British Isles. The Scottish Blackface is quite small but very hardy with its long, thick coat and lambs are born on the hillside. The ewes are fiercely protective of their lambs. The breed probably originated in the Borders and is known to have been in existence from at least the 16th century when James IV of Scotland developed or established a flock in the Ettrick Forest. All Blackface sheep have horns, a black or black and white face and black legs; they come in three types, the Perth type, the Lanark type and a soft-wooled Northumberland Blackface which is used in the breeding of the North of England Mule. The latter is a crossbreed where the sire is a Bluefaced Leicester ram and the dam is a Northumberland Blackface. Blackface sheep are farmed for their meat (Blackface lamb) and for their wool.[10]

A common feature to be seen across these upland areas is the circular sheepfold or 'stell'. They are scattered all over the hills and consist of a circular dry-stone, walled pen with a single, narrow entrance that could have been closed by a wooden gate, wicket or hurdle. They can be quite large, perhaps up to 30 feet in diameter with walls several feet thick and must survive from times gone by when shepherds lived in small huts up on the hills for many weeks at a time

A sheepfold or 'stell' in good condition and obviously still in use as it is close to the track at Snuffies Scar in the upper Breamish valley.

looking after their flocks. The stells might provide shelter for sheep in bad weather but this was probably not the main purpose as the hardy Borders sheep will hunker down behind stone walls, if there are any, or even in hollows in the ground where they can obtain some shelter from the wind and driving snow. The stells would have been used for holding sheep for such purposes as emergency first aid treatment or dipping or treating to protect against blowfly maggots, mites, ticks and lice, for dealing with foot rot and for removing 'daggy' wool from their rear ends. These high-level 'field stations' would have enabled sheep to be attended to without having to seek lower-level treatment at the farm. In some areas in the Border hills, there would also have been small stone-walled 'keb hooses' with corrugated iron roofs, used for sheltering sheep, carrying out emergency treatment, housing orphaned lambs and, with their fireplaces, for providing shelter for the shepherd and facilities for tea-brewing. Stells are often sited fairly close to water and this may have been for mixing up various potions and lotions.

There is very little woodland in the upper Breamish valley and, of this, any ancient woodland can only be found in steep-sided valleys and cleughs where it is protected from grazing and from human activity. In ancient times, oak probably grew up to a height of 500 m. (1,640 ft.). Now, in Northumberland National Park, ancient woodland (defined as woodland that has occupied a site since at least 1600AD) covers less than 1% of the land area. In Northumberland as a whole, 61% of ancient woodland (Ancient Semi-natural Woodland, 'ASNW' and Plantations on Semi-natural Woodland Sites, 'PAWS') is in an 'unfavourable declining' or 'partially destroyed' condition; 44% of ASNW is in an 'unfavourable declining' or 'partially destroyed' condition and 82% of PAWS is in a similar condition.

However, as a result of survey work done by the Northumberland Native Woodland Project in 2006 and initiated by the Forestry Commission, a *Native Woodland Habitat Action Plan* was drawn up for Northumberland in 2008 and an *Habitat Action Plan* has been drawn up for Northumberland National Park both of them putting forward a wide variety of measures for preventing further decline and encouraging the growth of ancient and native woodland.[11] Depending upon altitude, soil conditions and moisture levels, ancient woodland species include sessile and pendunculate oak, downy and silver birch, juniper, perhaps ash and alder in wetter areas and, at shrub level, hazel, holly and rowan. Juniper occurs on moorland as well as in woodland but is particularly at risk as it is not regenerating at many sites.

Half a mile below High Bleakhope farm, the R. Breamish

turns a sharp 90 degrees to the north-east at Low Bleakhope Farm. The hills rise steeply on either side below Low Cantle and the lower slopes of Shill Moor as the river flows between them to Snuffies Scar.

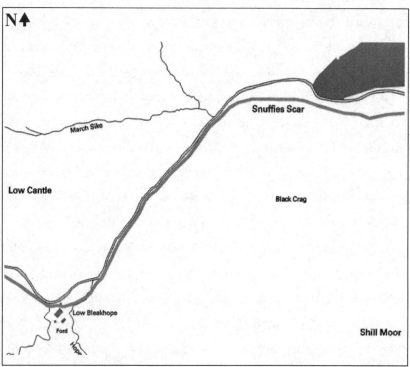

The distance between Low Bleakhope and the confluence with March Sike is about half a mile. Contains Ordnance Survey data © Crown copyright and database right 2014.

Because of the steep, narrow cleughs in the upland areas, a study was commissioned by the Food Animal Initiative in 2010, into the feasibility of micro hydro electricity at seven farms in the Cheviot Hills. Of these, five, including Low Bleakhope, were deemed to be feasible in engineering terms and would produce an economic return whilst, at the same time, reducing carbon emissions. All five were upland farms with high rainfall and a rugged terrain. Only one farm

34

was connected to the grid and, of the remainder, Low Bleakhope was considered to be the most promising off-grid site in the study with a possible pay-back time of between six and eight years. However, it was recognized that additional solar power might be needed in the summer when micro hydro would provide a smaller contribution to the electricity demand. It will be interesting to see how or whether micro hydro-electricity develops in the Cheviot Hills.

The rough road between Low Bleakhope and Snuffies Scar. This was taken on the walk up the valley so it is looking south-west towards Low Bleakhope Farm.

The R. Breamish flows in quite a narrow defile between Low Bleakhope and Snuffies Scar. Near the latter is a footbridge (see photo on next page) taking a footpath for sheep, shepherds and walkers that climbs up the side of March Sike past Low Cantle. Near the footbridge is a pole on which is sited a trap for mink. Any native

35

animal that enters the trap can be released unharmed but, if a mink is caught, it can be taken away for disposal. Such measures are necessary for the control and eradication of the American mink which is a non-native predatory species that first escaped from fur farms in the 1950s and 1960s and is a threat to native species such as water voles. Under the Wildlife and Countryside Act 1981, as amended, it is an offence to release mink into the wild and they have to be disposed of in a humane fashion.

Looking south-west from Snuffies Scar showing the footbridge and pole and the track leading up to High Cantle.

Snuffies Scar, around which the river turns to the east, is a strange name. I have not discovered its origin; perhaps there is a link between it and the name of the next descriptive shape of the course of the river at Snout End. I wonder whether both refer back to when wild boar roamed these hills in medieval times. But, I am probably way off beam. The track on the southern side of the river, rises across the lower northern slopes of Shill Moor. The track surface improves until, by Snout End, there is a good bitumen surface. The landscape is still wild and impressive but, east of Snuffies Scar, more woodland starts

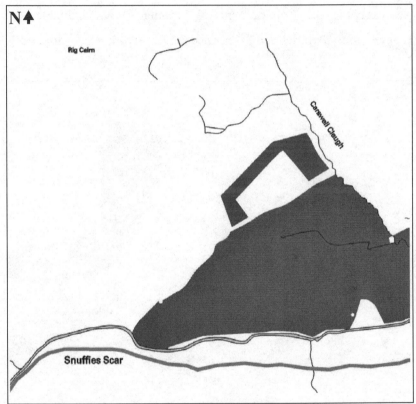

The solid grey line shows the track rising above and away from the river. The distance from west to east is about three-quarters of a mile. Contains Ordnance Survey data © Crown copyright and database right 2014.

to become apparent on the north side of the river. None of the woodland is natural and is a man-made addition to the landscape. Recent plantings between the river and the track will again change the landscape in years to come as will proposals by the Linhope Estate which, in September 2010 applied to the Forestry Commission for a woodland grant for new, native planting which will form part of the intended creation of 114 hectares of native woodland. The application was supported by the Northumberland National Park Authority which welcomed the estate's development of a Woodland Plan. This aims to increase the area of new native woodland for landscape and conservation purposes and to enhance the habitat for Black Grouse.

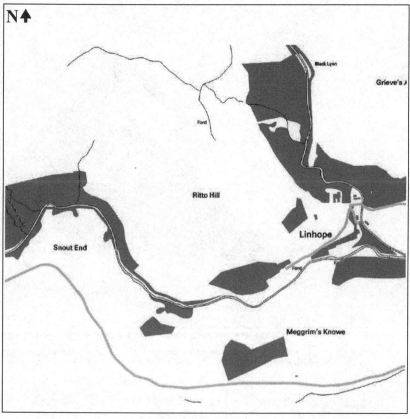

Continuation of map on p. 37. The distance from Snout End to Linhope is about three-quarters of a mile. Contains Ordnance Survey data © Crown copyright and database right 2014.

In the map on p. 37, the straight-sided block is a conifer plantation whilst the large shaded area on p. 37, extending eastwards opposite Snout End on p. 38, comprises native broadleaf trees and a mixture of native broadleaf trees and conifers.

Although not part of the woodland grant area, the estate intends to remove conifer blocks, including that at Carswell Cleugh, to form a more natural look to its woodlands, avoiding geometrical lines. Carswell Cleugh itself, is a particularly steep-sided ravine on a par with Cat Cleugh near High Bleakhope farm.

Looking east from Snout End down into the valley at Linhope and beyond.

The height of the track at Snout End is 320 m. (1,050 ft.), giving an impressive view to the east past Linhope towards Hartside (see above). This is such a prominent spot that there is an equally impressive view, but different in character, looking back towards Snuffies Scar with Low Cantle and High Cantle on the horizon.

The view from Snout End looking back towards Snuffies Scar. Note the stell beyond the trees in the middle distance.

At Snout End, the track veers away from the Breamish around the south side of the small hill of Meggrim's Knowe before dropping down to meet the river again at the farm of Alnhammoor. From now on, the valley floor and the hills on either side are peppered with ancient settlements and other features from different historical periods. A glance at the OS Explorer map OL 16 reveals settlements, homesteads, farmsteads, stones, cairns, cultivation terraces, enclosures, forts, hut circles and medieval villages, scattered over the whole of the eastern Cheviots. This book will mention some of them to be found on the way down the Breamish and Till valleys.

On Meggrim's Knowe, there are a series of earthworks that were probably a large settlement of Iron Age or Roman origin. A series of square and oval enclosures contain the remains of a number of round houses. On the other side of the river, there were prehistoric settlements and field systems on the side of Ritto Hill.[13]

In this book, I have resisted the temptation to venture up side valleys to look at tributaries and features associated with those tributaries but sometimes it is worth breaking the rule for something that the reader should not miss. One unmissable feature only requires a walk of little over a mile from Hartside, through the hamlet of Linhope, to reach Linhope Spout on the Linhope Burn. Linhope is, or was, a small hamlet; in 1825 Eneas Mackenzie describes it as standing:

> in a wild country, about 4 miles west from Ingram. At a little distance northward is *Linhope Spout*, or the *Roughting Linn*, so called from the great noise made by the fall of water after heavy rains; the word *Roughting* being also used by the

41

Borderers on hearing the lowing or bellowing of cattle. This cataract falling nearly 48 feet perpendicular, over a rugged rock of brown whin, spotted with green, makes a fine white sheet of foam. At the bottom is a bason [sic], seven feet in diameter, and fifteen feet in depth.....In this alpine region all the prominent features of nature still retain the descriptive appellations of the ancient Britons. *Linn*, in their language, denotes a pool formed below a waterfall—*Hope* signifies a vale, without a thoroughfare.....[14]

On the day when my companion and I were there, the sky was grey and mist was rolling in across the hills and valleys. There had been plenty of rain the day before and we could hear the roar of the waterfall long before we reached it. The path descends to the side of

The 'boiling' 'witches cauldron' below the waterfall of Linhope Spout.

42

the Spout with a view of the 'boiling', peaty water in the pool. The waterfall thunders into the pool from the left and the cold, turbulent water did not persuade us to indulge in any 'wild swimming'.

The impressive flow of Linhope Spout, a mixture of brown and white water.

In 1872, John Marius Wilson described how the:

Remains of an ancient fortified British town are at a spot called Greaves-Ash [on the hillside above Linhope]; and comprise three circular encampments, each with surrounding ramparts, enclosing perceptible foundations of houses. The W encampment is the largest, and has 18 hut-circles. A small silver cross, inscribed with the name of Acca, Bishop of Hexham, and thought to have been one of the crosses given to the Hexham pilgrims, was found, in 1861, at the foot of the adjoining Cheviot hill Hartside.[15]

A later record states that the site was excavated in 1861 when a glass arm ring was found. The site could have been Iron Age in date, with occupation probably continuing into the Roman period.[16]

Alnhammoor farm is an old farm and there are remains of a ruined farmstead nearby near the junction between the Shank Burn and the Breamish that predate the present 19th century farm buildings. There are also some old, dry-stone walls that may be associated with it. *Aln* (as in R. Alne, Alnmouth, Alnwick) may derive from some Celtic or Gaelic adjective, *aluin*, *alainne*, *ailne*, meaning 'fair', 'handsome' or Welsh *alain*, *alwyn*, meaning 'bright', 'clear', 'lucid'. *Ham* derives from Old English for 'home' or 'settlement'. The 'fair house on the moor' seems an apt description.[17]

At Alnhammoor, there is a bridge over the Breamish capable of taking vehicles, although, as with the bridge higher up the valley at High Bleakhope, these are private vehicles because public traffic is not permitted beyond Hartside, east of Linhope, where walkers' cars are parked on the grass verge. According to old OS maps, the bridge was a footbridge until about 1980; before the present bridge was built, vehicles used fords slightly further up the river, near the confluence of the Shank Burn with the R. Breamish.

The modern, private bridge over the R. Breamish at Alnhammoor built of railway sleepers on RSJs, concrete piers and timber and tubular handrails.

From Alnhammoor, the Breamish flows round the back of Hartside Hill, quite a lump of a hill, which is topped by ancient settlements, homesteads and cairns. The earlier settlement of stone circles has been judged to be of Roman date and two large enclosures contain the foundations of what may have been medieval buildings. The cairns are described as 'Shepherd's Cairns'.[18] The river then flows north between Hartside Hill and Brough Law past the Ingram Glidders; these are impressive scree slopes on the side of Brough Law that are tackled in an annual, short, hard, fell race of 0.9 mile.

45

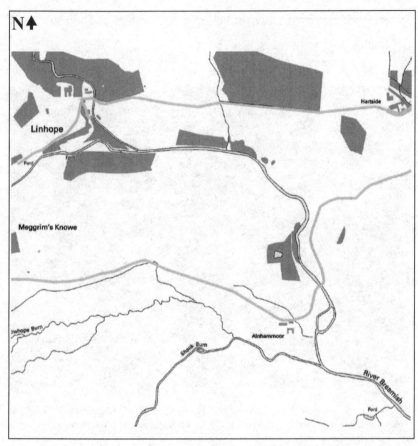

Map showing Linhope and Alnhammoor; the distance between them is about three-quarters of a mile, as the crow flies. Contains Ordnance Survey data © Crown copyright and database right 2014.

From the Ingram Glidders, the river turns north-east passing underneath the first substantial road bridge, the attractive, 'Peggy Bell's Bridge'. This was built in 1908 of reinforced concrete with ribbed arches, having a span of 52 ft. 6 in. The bridge was built using the 'Hennebique', a pioneering system of reinforced concrete invented by a French engineer in the late 19th century.

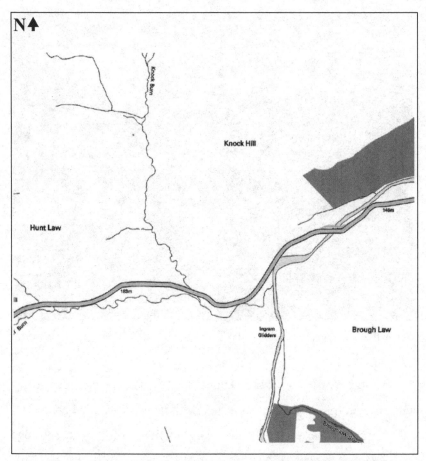

The river swings north-east under Peggy Bell's Bridge below Brough Law. Hartside Hill is to the west of Ingram Glidders (from Anglo-Saxon *glídan* meaning 'slippery'). The distance from west to east across the map is about one mile. Contains Ordnance Survey data © Crown copyright and database right 2014.

Peggy Bell's bridge was considerably refurbished between 2008 and 2010 as it was seriously under strength and looking run down. The arches and deck of the bridge were renewed and the abutments refurbished but the old shape of the bridge was retained. Despite the work being hampered by flooding, the bridge was opened

Peggy Bell's Bridge, Breamish Valley.

in October 2010, by Lord James Percy. The bridge can carry unrestricted traffic and is picturesque with its white-painted parapets.

Tony Dickens tells the story in 1975 of how the bridge received its name:

> Apparently, in the winter of 1906, a young maid who was in service at Great Ryle, had decided to make her way home during a storm which had brought the river Breamish into full flood. Before the present bridge was constructed the river at this point was spanned by a wooden trestle type bridge and, as the young maid crossed this bridge, it suddenly collapsed and pitched her into the river where she was tragically drowned. The young maid was called Peggy Bell, and when

the present bridge was erected it was in her memory that it was named.[19]

Brough Law is topped by an impressive hillfort with surviving stone ramparts. To the south and east are more forts and settlements at Turf Knowe, Middle Dean, Wether Hill and Ingram Hill. All around, there are obvious signs of cultivation terraces that date from prehistoric, medieval and more recent times. Brough Law is easily accessible by a grassy track from the car park at Bulby's Wood and many of the hillforts can be reached by a hillfort trail, waymarked by the Northumberland National Park Authority.

Excavations were first carried out on the archaeology of the valley in the 1860s by the antiquarian, George Tate, who examined sites including Brough Law and Greaves Ash. Further work was done by A. H. A. Hogg in the 1930s and by George Jobey in 1970. From 1994 until 2004, the Breamish Valley Archaeology Project (BVA), a joint venture between the Northumberland National Park Authority, Durham University and the Northumberland Archaeology Group (NAG), carried out summer excavations on Breamish Valley sites. The basis for BVA's work was a survey carried out by the Royal Commission on Historical Monuments for England during the 1980s. More recently, further excavations have been undertaken at Wether Hill.

A great deal of information has been obtained from the many sites and much of this is available in readable form.[20] Turf Knowe produced Bronze Age burial cairns with cremations and stone cists. Food and burial vessels were found there and a collection of jet beads. Other artefacts showed that occupation or human presence continued

49

into the Iron Age or beyond. Middle Dean has earthen ramparts and evidence of round houses, Ingram Hill has a set of double ditches from the Iron Age with later, rectangular, stone buildings and Wether Hill has shallow, circular ditches with the remains of timber roundhouses.

Brough Law has the most commanding and dramatic position of all the forts and its massive walls are particularly impressive. The walls have mostly tumbled but a small section that has survived intact from the Iron Age shows meticulous construction. The excavations in 1999 included a single, excavation trench across a dyke or wall going across the ridge that was built to control movement approaching the fort from the south. Charcoal dated the dyke to 210 BC; both dyke and hillfort were built at the same time.

Brough Law ramparts, looking east.

Space does not permit a discussion on the considerable archaeological work that has been carried out in the upper Breamish valley and Northumberland National Park since the 1860s and contained in many academic site reports and research papers but, apart from these, the reader who wishes to move on from the excellent publications by the Northumberland National Park Authority will find a great deal of information in the very comprehensive, *An Archaeological Research Framework for Northumberland National Park*. The Framework brings together a series of discussion papers with fascinating information on what has been discovered so far, which are used as a 'flexible structure for decision making in relation to archaeological research within the National Park'.[21]

It is the artefacts mentioned in the many academic and other documents that particularly fire our imagination. For example, the Alnham Village Atlas records:

> The bronze spearhead found at High Bleakhope (Site. [1] NT 920150) is perhaps of similar type to the spearhead with lunate openings in the blade from the Whittingham hoard (Cowen 1935, 28). Bronze weapons such as this are extremely rare, and are likely to have been very valuable, perhaps the exclusive preserve of an elite social class (Higham 1986, 104). Though the circumstances and exact provenance of this find are unknown, High Bleakhope occupies an elevated and remote position. This may indicate that the spear may have been deliberately deposited, perhaps as an offering to a deity, rather than accidentally lost. As in the preceding Neolithic, religion and ritual was extremely

51

important in Bronze Age society, and this is reflected in the complex burial traditions of the period.[22]

Another example is a Bronze Age cauldron found at Alnhammoor. This was buried in a wet area and there is evidence to suggest that, after the climate became wetter, c. 1200 BC, valuable bronze objects were deposited in bogs and pools, not just in the National Park, but throughout Britain. These objects may have been gifts to the gods, perhaps associated with the scattering of funeral pyre ashes.[25]

The R. Breamish looking upstream at Bulby's Wood picnic area and car park.

From Bulby's Wood, below Brough Law, the river runs east and then skirts the village of Ingram on the north side before flowing below Ingram Bridge. In summer, as the road reaches the village from the west, it enters a long, dark-green 'tunnel' formed by the overhanging trees. Ingram consists of buildings laid out on either side of the road and a separate, smaller group of buildings to the east, which includes the church and the vicarage.

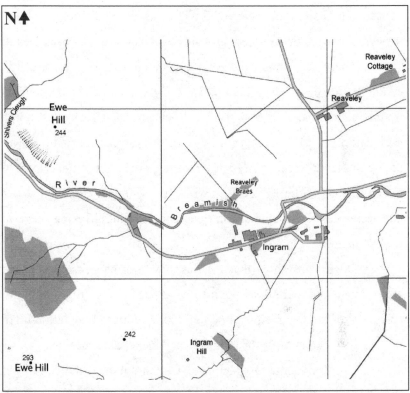

Ingram Village, the northern 'gateway' to Northumberland National Park. Each grid is 1 sq.km. Contains Ordnance Survey data © Crown copyright and database right 2014.

Documents relating to the history of the village date back to the early medieval era; perhaps the earliest is *The Historia de Sancto Cuthberto* or 'History of St. Cuthbert' which was probably written in the 10th century and which states that the monastery of Lindisfarne owned all the land (which must have included Ingram and the wider

53

area) on either side of the R. Breamish right up to its source.[24] The manor of Ingram with cottages, gardens and arable land, meadow, forge, a mill and a brewhouse was held by Geoffrey de Lucy until his death in 1284. The make-up of the village seems to have been much the same in 1353 on the death of Sir Thomas Heton although many of the cottages were unoccupied, probably as a result of the Black Death.

There was, and still is, a parish church and, by the 16th century, a tower or bastle held by Lord Ogle, that was later occupied by the rector. The earliest part of St Michael and All Angels Church may date back to the 11th century with the lower part of the tower dating to the 12th century. The nave, aisles, arcades and upper part of the tower date to the 13th century with changes and additions made in later centuries and major restorations and rebuilding taking place in the 19th century.

Documents show that farming practices had changed by the 18th century and there does seem to have been a shift from arable to pasture after the late medieval period with a reduced population often living in poor conditions. In 1825, Eneas Mackenzie states that:

> INGRAM is a small village situated south of the Breamish, two miles west from the turnpike road, and $9\frac{1}{2}$ miles south from Wooler. The church is dedicated to St. Michael, and the living is a rectory, valued in the king's books at £24, 16s. 8d. This place is the property of John Collingwood Tarleton, Esq.[25]

The Northumberland County Histories give information on the different townships or 'vills' encompassed by Ingram parish from medieval times. By the mid 18th century, the parish comprised, in three divisions, the townships of Ingram, Greenside Hill, Grieve's Ash, Lynhope, Standrope, Faldon, the Clinch, Hartside and Reeveley; the south side of the valley had been previously incorporated into Alnham parish.[26] Because the earliest detailed map of Ingram is an estate map of 1820, the layout of the village before that date is conjectural, with the exception of the church and, probably, the water-powered corn mill which may well have always been on the site still marked on the current OS map, downstream of the village.

In 2001 as part of the Breamish Valley Archaeology Project, there were excavations in the Ingram Rectory Gardens in order to look for traces of early medieval settlement. No evidence of this was found but more than 600 sherds of medieval pottery were discovered dating from the 12th and 13th centuries that were thought to have been left over from the manuring of rig and furrow fields. Little dating evidence was found from later centuries which suggests that the fields had been switched from arable to pasture by the 14th century.[27]

As the R. Breamish flows beneath Ingram Bridge (Grid Ref: NU01741640), it leaves the Northumberland National Park. The terrain changes at this point from the mountainous areas of the Cheviot Hills to the lower-lying agricultural lands to the east. The village of Ingram is regarded as an important gateway to the National Park, a status that used to be reflected in the former National Park Visitor Centre that closed in 2012.

Tony Dickens' description of Ingram Bridge in 1975 states that:

It is a lattice girder bridge, and has two span metal joists with troughing to its deck. There is a plaque on the bridge which states it was built in 1893 by the Cleveland Bridge and Engineering Company of Darlington. The span of the metal joists are 61 feet 6 inches with a single pier and its height is 13 feet 6 inches with 5 feet parapets and a width between parapets of 12 feet. The name of Ingram is of some considerable antiquity and it means "In yore folk".[28]

When Peggy Bell's bridge was rebuilt following the floods of 2008 and 2009, Ingram Bridge was strengthened at the same time but its appearance and structure has not changed to any great extent since 1893.

Ingram Bridge from the upstream side.

3

Ingram Bridge to Bewick Bridge

After leaving Ingram Bridge, the Breamish flows past the site of one of the former water mills, downstream of the village. There was a mill mentioned in the *Inquisitions Post Mortem* of Geoffrey de Lucy in 1284 and Geoffrey Heton in 1353. The 1860 OS map shows it as a corn mill but it seems to have gone out of use after that.[1]

Looking west from Ingram Bridge towards the village.

East and west of the bridge, the river has a meandering course and, over the years, this has shifted from side to side within the obvious gravel beds. Low-growing vegetation such as broom and gorse cover the banks and it is worth looking out for the attractive, bright yellow, monkey-flower, *Mimulus guttatus*.

Downstream, the steep-sided Heddon Hill overlooks the north bank of the river and the confluence with the Reaveley Burn. The cultivation terraces on the west and south slopes stand out very well, particularly when shadows are formed in afternoon and evening sunlight. The terraces were made by medieval or earlier, ploughmen; horizontal terraces conform to the contours of the hill whereas other 'vertical' strips are laid out at right angles to them, looking as though they are later in date because they seem to cut across them. Medieval farmers used the 'open field system' with each farmer having his own strip of land, separated from his neighbour's by an unploughed 'baulk'. It may be that the horizontal terraces are prehistoric in origin or that the medieval terraces are overlaid on earlier systems.[2]

The proliferation of cultivation terraces and settlement remains dating from prehistoric and Roman times through to the medieval period or, quite often, post-medieval period, confirm that the population of the area was much higher than it is today. The positioning of the cultivation strips and terraces on the hillsides suggests that arable land was not easily available down in the valleys because of undrained marshland and thick vegetation.

Opposite Heddon Hill, on the south side of the river is the higher, East Hill, the configuration of which, including its steep slopes, has made it attractive as a hang-gliding site.

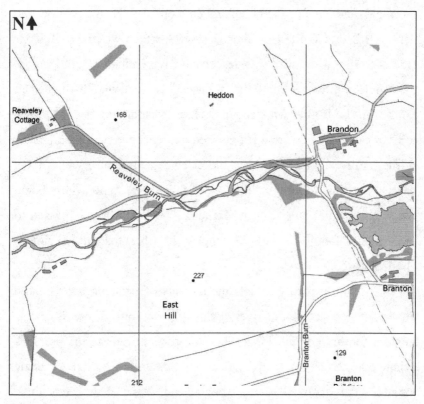

Map showing the R. Breamish flowing east from Ingram and between the villages of Brandon and Branton. 1 sq.km. grids. Contains Ordnance Survey data © Crown copyright and database right 2014.

The hamlet of Brandon is really one farm and tied cottages with what was once a blacksmith's shop. A lade shows that there once was a mill and there are the remains of a chapel first recorded in 1432 when the vicar of Eglingham was punished for not appointing a priest. The chapel was in ruins by the mid 17th century although the graveyard was used for burials until the early 19th century. The ruins were partly repaired in 1903 and the graveyard cleared out. Part of a 12th century font was found. The chapel is a Scheduled Monument.[3]

In 1825, Eneas Mackenzie described Brandon as 'one farmhold and about sixteen inhabited houses'.[4] He mentioned the nearby Brandon White House on the A697, which was the seat of Sir Daniel Collingwood who was descended from Cuthbert Collingwood, the 'renowned Border chieftain' in the 16th century who distinguished himself in the Border wars and was chaplain and, later, sword-bearer to Charles II. There were distinguished descendants in many branches of the family at Lilburn Tower and elsewhere; the most well-known descendant was Admiral Collingwood of Trafalgar fame, whose home was Collingwood House near Morpeth. The White House passed to the Allgood family in the 17th century; it still stands and is now a Grade II listed building.

A minor road connects the hamlets of Brandon and Branton on opposite sides of the river, by way of a ford. There is also a modern footbridge built high above the river to replace the previous bridge that was swept away by floods in September 2008. Mackenzie mentions the small village of Branton and says that, in 1825, there was 'a neat Presbyterian meeting-house, and a respectable seminary kept by the Rev. N. Blyth, M.A. Some antiquarians have supposed that this is the Roman station *Bremenium*'. The antiquarians were mistaken as Bremenium is a considerable distance away on the Roman road of Dere Street, at High Rochester, near Otterburn.

Brandon and Branton may be no more than hamlets yet William Camden was aware of their existence when, in 1610, he wrote:

> ...the streame of Till, a river that hath two names. For at the head, which is in the innermore part of the country, it is called

Bramish, and upon it standeth Bramton [Branton], a little village, very obscure and almost of no reckoning; from whence it goeth Northward by Bengeley [Beanley], which together with Bampton it selfe, with Broundum [Brandon], Rodam (which hath given name to a stock in this tract of goode note), Edelingham &., was in King Henrie the Third his time the Baronie of Patricke Earle of Dunbar...[5]

Ford and modern footbridge linking Brandon with Branton.

Branton Quarry, formerly operated by Cemex, used to be situated to the north of the river, to the west of Powburn. A sand and gravel process area associated with the Breamish Quarry was to the north of the R. Breamish. Extraction, which has now ceased, took place over eleven phases with a progressive restoration programme to form two large lakes, a fishing lake and a conservation lake. More than 1.66 M. tonnes of sand gravel were extracted from 1996 until closure. The lakes were then constructed and a 29 hectares nature and wildlife reserve was opened in October 2011. The Northumberland National Park Authority donated a bird hide which is used by the Northumberland Bird Club as well as other bird-watchers; more than 140 species of birds and wildlife have been spotted on the restored site which is still owned by Cemex.

Birds to be seen include waders such as oystercatcher, lapwing, little ringed plover and curlew (the emblem of Northumberland National Park). Wildfowl include tufted duck, mallard, coot and shelduck; greylag and Canada geese both breed on site. Around the fringes, reed bunting, thrush, blackbird, heron, sand martin and perhaps a kingfisher may be seen and black-headed gulls can be seen on the island. Plants include ox-eye daisy, *Leucanthemum vulgare*; yellow rattle, *Rhinanthus minor*; devils-bit scabious, *Succisa pratensis*; buttercup, *Ranunculus*; wood cranesbill, *Geranium sylvaticum*; yellow flag iris, *Iris pseudacorus*; marsh marigold, *Caltha palustris*; forget-me-not, *Myosotis sylvatica*; branched bur-reed, *Sparganium erectum* and reedmace, *Typha latifolia*.

Otters have been seen in the river and the lakes are home to frogs, toads, the common hawker dragonfly and common blue damselfly. It is encouraging that a number of plants on the *North Northumberland, Scarce, Rare & Extinct Vascular Plant Register* have been introduced to the conservation lake and seem to be thriving.[6] Our visit on a warm, summer day provided convincing proof of the benefits of conservation as applied to former gravel pits.

The conservation lake, Branton, with ox-eye daisies and other wild flowers.

To the east of Branton lakes, the Breamish flows beneath Hedgeley Bridge which carries the main A697 road. The bridge was built in 1970 of precast concrete, replacing a lattice girder bridge built in 1892 that was similar to Ingram Bridge. There were earlier bridges, one of which was recorded by John Wallis in 1769:

> We cross the *Bramish* [sic] by a new stone-bridge, above which, on the right hand, and in sight, is Branton...[7]

The bridge was short-lived, as two arches were washed away by floods in 1772; the County Council invited tenders for a replacement in 1765.[8]

There was major damage to the foundations of the bridge during flooding in 2010 when a weir collapsed causing a scour pool on the downstream side. After emergency work to stabilize the bridge, permanent repairs were carried out in 2011 that included an extra concrete apron across the entire width of the river and a stepped fish pass to help otters, eels and migrating fish.

The repairs were estimated to cost £400,000 and the fish pass, £150,000.[9]

Hedgeley Bridge from the east showing the concrete apron. Grid Ref. NU05861710. The stepped fish pass is behind the shutters to the right.

There is a conjunction of transport and history in the vicinity of Hedgeley Bridge. The straight section of the A697 to the north of the bridge, lies along the route of the Devil's Causeway, a Roman road that branched off Dere Street north of Corbridge and headed for Berwick-upon-Tweed, probably to take advantage of harbour facilities for supporting the first Roman advance into Scotland under

Agricola in the 1st century and the Antonine and Severan campaigns in the 2nd and 3rd centuries.

Just east of Hedgeley Bridge are the piers of the old railway bridge that carried the North Eastern Railway's branch line from Alnwick through Wooler to Cornhill-on-Tweed. The line opened in 1887 but was closed to passengers in 1930 and for freight in 1953, the closing company being the London and North Eastern Railway. The station was built at Hedgeley rather than at Powburn because the local landowner, Captain R. Carr-Ellison, with others, had agreed to make land available at favourable rates. Hedgeley Station has been converted into two private houses and the track infilled but the station forecourt is still visible as a drive-in area in front of the houses.[10]

Looking east from Hedgeley Bridge showing the stepped fish pass. One of the railway bridge piers is just visible in the middle distance.

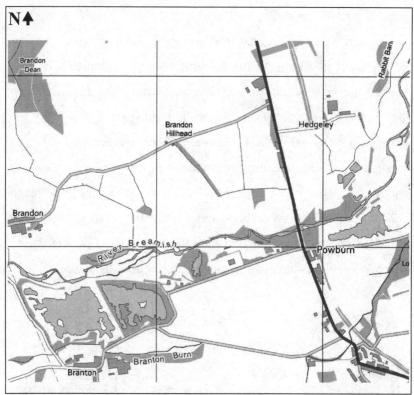

Hedgeley Bridge is just north of Powburn. The A697 road is shown by heavy black line. 1 sq.km. grid squares. Contains Ordnance Survey data © Crown copyright and database right 2014.

There are two current or completed sand and gravel extraction areas east of Hedgeley Bridge at Hedgeley and Low Hedgeley. At Hedgeley, over 1 M. tonnes is still being extracted by North East Concrete Ltd over a seven year period with restoration thereafter to a mixture of agriculture and nature conservation including areas of shallow water. Earlier quarrying activities by Cemex occurred at Low Hedgeley the planning permission for which allowed the extraction of up to 1 M. tonnes, progressively worked over four phases. The restoration includes two large lakes with agricultural land in between, drainage, tree planting, a bird hide and other landscaping work. A sluice at the discharge end of the eastern lake allows water levels to be controlled to encourage migrant waders and wildfowl.[11]

Compliance with statutory regulations is paramount and planning applications for quarrying activities have to be accompanied by Environmental Impact Statements in accordance with the Town & Country Planning (Environmental Impact Assessment) Regulations 1999 and they have to satisfy the requirements of The Conservation of Habitats and Species Regulations 2010.

All activities along the Breamish and Till valleys are subject to stringent controls because the valleys are within the River Tweed Special Area of Conservation (SAC) which recognizes the presence of aquatic plant communities, insects, Atlantic salmon and otter, sea lamprey, brook lamprey and river lamprey. The rivers and their tributaries are also designated as the nationally important Tweed Catchment Rivers (England: Till Catchment) Site of Special Scientific Interest (SSSI). This is because the Till Catchment forms part of the River Tweed system which includes rivers with clean water and having high conservation and ecological value.[12]

The environmental importance of the Till Catchment SSSI and the need to restore, improve and maintain the condition of the rivers is reflected in the *River Till Restoration Strategy* drawn up by Natural England, the Environment Agency and the Tweed Forum in March 2013.[13] This is a detailed and ambitious strategy that identifies the current condition of the rivers, sets out the potential solutions, costs the solutions and says how they are to be delivered over a 25-50 year timescale. The lead organizations for delivery are Natural

England and the Environment Agency and both will report to DEFRA with the exception of the upper Bowmont Water, which comes under Scottish jurisdiction.

Looking at an overview of the seven units within the SSSI, all of them are classified as 'unfavourable' in condition. Four of them are classified as 'unfavourable no change', two of them as 'unfavourable recovering' and one is 'unfavourable declining'. The reasons for failure include inappropriate weirs, dams and other structures, invasive freshwater species and water pollution from agricultural run-off. Solutions include a detailed range of measures under the general headings of:

1. Allowing natural recovery
2. Assisted natural recovery
3. Recognising and implementing protocols for river management by working with 'stakeholders'
4. Channel corridor methods such as allowing space for the river to move
5. Riparian measures such as the rehabilitation of river banks and bankside habitats
6. In-channel measures such as removing or modifying engineered structures

Under these headings, the actions proposed range from major, hard engineering works to river bank management, planting trees, creating wet areas, removing barriers to fish migration, establishing grazing regimes, reducing pollution and much more.

All the actions need to be compatible with other objectives such as those of the Water Framework Directive (WFD).

68

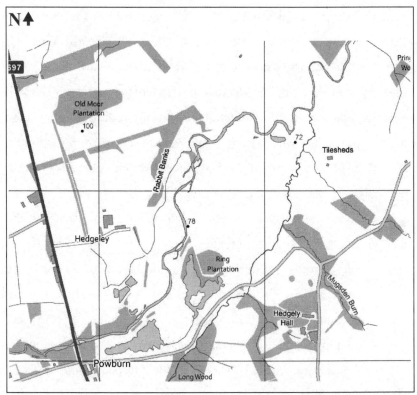

The R. Breamish meanders north-east from Hedgeley Hall. 1 sq.km. grids. Contains Ordnance Survey data © Crown copyright and database right 2014.

Allen Mawer gives the derivation of 'Hedgeley' as 'Hiddi's clearing'. He mentions several medieval spellings, the earliest, from around 1150, being *Hiddesleie* in the *Percy Chartulary* (the archives of the Earls of Northumberland). There is no clue as to who was 'Hiddi' but 'ley' is from the OE, *leah*, meaning a tract of open ground.[14]

Hedgeley gives its name to Hedgeley Moor, a mile or so to the north that was the site of a battle in 1464 during the Wars of the Roses. Lord Montague had been sent to guide emissaries of James III

69

of Scotland through Northumberland which was held by his enemies, the Lancastrians. Lord Montague's forces were attacked by Sir Ralph Percy but the latter was defeated and killed. The nearby Grade II listed, Percy's Cross, which is still there on the east side of the A697 road, was erected in the 15th century to commemorate Sir Ralph Percy's death.[15] I am straying slightly from my route again but these nearby places and events are too important to leave out. So is the St. James' Well just south of Percy's Cross, which was a holy well, probably associated with a medieval chapel at Wooperton.

There are many holy wells in Northumberland. In 1878, the Rev. G. Rome Hall suggested that:

Sacred wells, for our purpose, are of *three* kinds:—(1) Those connected with Christian places of worship or holy personages of early Christian times; (2) ordinary springs, but held in special estimation; and (3) medicinal or mineral wells. All these are usually known in their respective localities as "Holy Wells"...[16]

Many of these wells were the subject of ceremonies carried out by villagers, such as the 'dressing' of a well with flowers; the purpose of this might be a celebration of the perceived benefits provided by the well and its water and a way of ensuring that the benefit would endure in the future. The sacred water might have been used for baptisms and ceremonies would often have originated much earlier, in pagan times. Votive offerings were also made in the form of small objects or coins in order to seek some benefit for the individual. The medicinal properties of certain wells would have given them sacred status if it were believed that they had miraculous powers. Similarly, if folklore

INGRAM BRIDGE TO BEWICK BRIDGE

maintained that a holy person (such as the wandering St. Cuthbert in Northumberland) had drunk from the well, then the waters, even though not having medicinal minerals, would be assumed to have miraculous powers. In 1893, Robert Charles Hope described 28 wells and three superstitions relating to rivers in Northumberland although he did not mention St. James' Well.[17]

History is everywhere here. There are earthworks east of Low Hedgeley Farm that are the deserted remains of a medieval village. There are signs of ridge and furrow agriculture on either side of the river and on rising ground between Hedgeley and Beanley and beyond. A Second World War pillbox still survives between Hedgeley Bridge and the railway bridge pier on the north bank.

The Hedgeley Estate extends to approximately 1,640 hectares (4,053 acres) of which 1,272 hectares (3,143 acres) forms Hedgeley Farms, consisting of arable land, grassland, moorland and forestry. Since 2006, the Farms have built up a herd of pedigree Galloway and Belted Galloway cows, North Country Mule ewes and Swaledale and Blackface sheep. The estate has been owned by the Carr-Ellison family of Hedgeley Hall since 1786.

The R. Breamish meanders north-east from the restored gravel workings through open pasture. There are permissive footpaths and bridleways crossing the river or running alongside it in places. There is an old track running south-east from Low Hedgeley that crosses the river by a ford and heads in the direction of Hedgeley Hall round the side of Ring Plantation. The low pasture provides a habitat for lapwings and oyster catchers and the river banks are home to sand martins. High above the new lakes, is Hedgeley Hall, set in parkland

and woods. It is a Grade II listed building that largely replaced an earlier house that was there before Sir Ralph Carr purchased the estate in 1786. The house was altered and added to in the 19th and 20th centuries.

The south-west aspect from the house looks uphill towards Crawley Farm and the Grade II listed Crawley Tower, an early 14th century tower, the ruins of which had a cottage built inside it during the 18th century. The name probably derives from *Caer-law* meaning 'castle hill' or 'fortified hill', *Caer* from the Brythonic language endemic to the lands south of the Forth estuary in Iron Age and Roman times and *law* from the Scots for 'hill'. The tower, which would have been surrounded by other fortifications, is an impressive structure with massive masonry and has been in the ownership of the Carr-Ellison family since 1931. The tower can be seen from the road but neither it nor Hedgeley Hall is open to the public. Nearby earthworks shown on the OS map consist of an outer rampart and an inner platform and are possibly the remains of an Iron Age/Roman settlement.[18]

The R. Breamish flows to the north-west of the village of Beanley from where old tracks lead north-west and south-west to cross the river by several fords. The south-west track eventually links up with the track from Low Hedgeley mentioned on the previous page. In 1870-72, John Marius Wilson describes Beanley as being:

> a township in Eglingham parish, Northumberland; on the river Breamish, 7 miles NW of Alnwick. Acres, 2,341. Pop., 116. Houses, 23. The earls of Dunbar anciently held it on the tenure of maintaining a road into Scotland...[19]

In 1825, Eneas Mackenzie had said that, in old records, Beanley was generally spelt *Ben-ley* 'probably composed of the Gaelic, *ben*, a mountain, and *ley*, pasture'.[20]

One of a number of fords along this stretch. This one is west of Beanley village at Grid.Ref. NU07171845. A footbridge shown on the OS map has now gone.

Mackenzie also refers to Gallow Law, which is still shown on the modern OS map on the northern side of the Breamish, as being 'the place of execution for the barony of Beanley'. This is north-east of Rabbit Banks but not shown on the map on p. 74. He also mentions 'the remains of a British camp with a double fosse and rampart' on the summit of Beanley Plantation. Modern records show two Iron Age forts on the east side of the minor road that runs along the west side of Beanley Moor and Plantation. However, Mackenzie may have been referring to The Ringses Camp nearby, described in *Archaeologia*

Aeliana in 1882 as 'having a double foss [sic] and rampart. The road leading from it is still very perfect, winding down the declivity of the hill, and guarded with large stones placed edgeways'.[21]

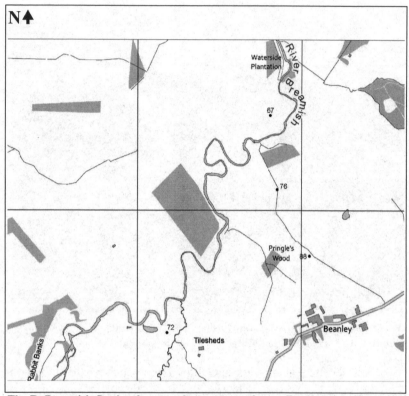

The R. Breamish flowing from south-west to north past Beanley. 1 sq.km. grids. Contains Ordnance Survey data © Crown copyright and database right 2014. The Ringses and other forts or camps (not shown on this map) are to the east of Beanley—see OS map 332.

The position of The Ringses camp, overlooked by higher ground, suggests that it might have been a fortified settlement rather than a high level fort but, whatever its purpose, the ramparts and protected entrances are impressive. It is probably Iron Age or Roman in date.[22]

74

In Beanley village, there is the site of a medieval village on the south side of the village street, next to Beanley Hall. To the west of the village alongside the track leading to the ford in the photograph on p. 73 is the site of Beanley Tile Works with a clay pit next to it. The Works ceased production sometime after 1862.[23] The tileyard was where 'Tilesheds' is shown on the map on p. 74, now Gamekeeper's Cottage.

The Scots Peerage in 1906 relates how Cospatrick, the 2nd Earl of Dunbar was granted Beanley by King Henry I, sometime between 1100 and 1136 as part of a large tract of land between Wooler and Morpeth. Unusually, it was not held by knight's service (i.e. under service to fight for the king when called upon) but was held in grand serjeanty (another feudal tenure requiring a service rather than a rent) that bound Cospatrick and his descendants to be 'inborwe' and 'utborwe' between England and Scotland. This meant that all travellers to or from Scotland had to obtain permission from the lords of Beanley. Other lands at Eglingham, Bewick, Hedgeley, Edlingham, Harehope and elsewhere were owned by Cospatrick and his sons but, in 1160-61, his son Cospatrick, the 3rd Earl, paid 12 marks to the English Exchequer for six knights' fees; he had apparently commuted the service due from him for Beanley.[24]

The 3rd Earl Cospatrick, having inherited his father's lands in Scotland as well as the serjeanty of Beanley, then paid more attention to his Scottish interests that were of more importance to him and gave grants to religious houses in Scotland; it was he who founded the nunnery at Coldstream where, according to *The Scots Peerage*, 'there was already a small religious house'.[25]

Eneas Mackenzie refers to Beanley as being:

the barony of the Earls of Dunbar, the descendants of the illustrious Gospatric, the expatriated Earl of Northumberland. The 5th Earl's estates in Northumberland were forfeited to Edward III in 1309 and remained with the Crown until Edward III granted them to Henry Percy in 1334 'for ever'.[26]

Beanley is now part of the Hedgeley Estate in Hedgeley Parish and Beanley Hall is occupied by members of the Carr-Ellison family.

After leaving the environs of Beanley, the river meanders north and north-west, passing Scar Brae (where there are obvious signs of bank scouring) and Waterside Plantation towards New Bewick Bridge. The river from Hedgeley Bridge to New Bewick Bridge and beyond sees numbers of small, named and unnamed tributaries entering the river although the river itself (except when in spate) is still shallow enough to be crossed by fords and narrow footbridges.

A ford and footbridge upstream of Scar Brae at Grid Ref. NU07711940.

The footbridge in the photograph, which has replaced an older one (vestiges of the piers remain), carries a public footpath from below Titlington Pike, through Beanley to New Bewick Bridge. Just before reaching New Bewick Bridge, there is a glimpse across the river to Harehope Hall which is surrounded on three sides by woodland and has an open aspect on the south-west side. A track from the Hall leads down to an old, unused-looking ford across the river.

Summer vegetation only allows a glimpse of Harehope Hall across the river.

J. C. Hodgson tells us that Harehope was one of the manors granted by Henry I to Cospatric in 1135. In 1178, Cospatric III's nephew, Waldeve, granted Harehope to the brethren of St. Lazarus who owned a hospital for lepers in Leicestershire.[27] There was a hospital at Harehope by 1230 and it continued until the dissolution of religious houses and hospitals under Henry VIII who granted

Harehope to Henry Mountjoy. His heirs, Lord Mountjoy and his wife, sold it in 1567 to Luke Ogle. Subsequent owners during the 17th and 18th centuries include the Storey family and the Forsters until, in 1755, Harehope was bought by Mary Harvey of Newcastle who also inherited the estate of Bewick. Tony Dickens says that on the eastern slope of Harehope Hill, 'a tank like structure has been cut into the rock and was supposed to have been used by the Storey family in the 17th or 18th century for the manufacture of gin from juniper berries.'[28]

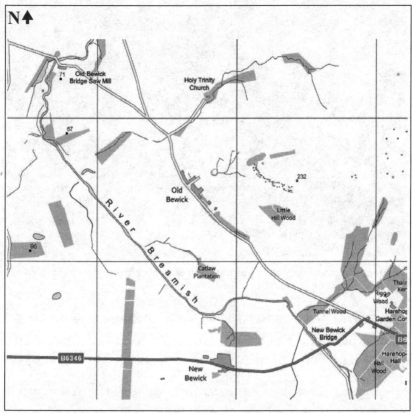

The R. Breamish flows north-west between New Bewick Bridge and Old Bewick Bridge. 1 sq.km. grids. Contains Ordnance Survey data © Crown copyright and database right 2014.

Harehope, Old Bewick, New Bewick and East Lilburn were purchased in 1830 by Mr. A J. Cresswell of Cresswell and the foundation stone of Harehope Hall was laid in 1846 by Mr. Cresswell's grandson, Oswin, aged a year and a half.[29] Harehope Hall was completed in 1848 as a shooting lodge for the Cresswell family who had been major landowners elsewhere in Northumberland since the reign of King John. The unlisted Hall and the estate eventually passed to the Wrangham family and, in 2012, was offered for sale with its lodge, stable block and outbuildings, gardens, three acres of paddock, 53 acres of woodland and 26 acres of farmland.

The modern bridge at New Bewick, looking north-east. Grid Ref. NU07622040.

In 1975, Tony Dickens says that the 'rather insignificant bridge' carrying the B6346 was built in 1882 by P & W. McLean at their Clutha Iron Works in Glasgow and was strengthened in 1930.[30] However, its bow and plate girders and jack arches have recently been replaced by concrete beams and modern parapet railings. The road links the settlement of New Bewick on the south-west side of the river with Old Bewick on the north-east side of the river. Aerial photographs located the site of an Anglo Saxon village at New Bewick showing boundaries, enclosures and a small building with a sunken floor; some of the features were excavated in the 1980s and finds included loom weights and pottery.

From just before New Bewick Bridge, the R. Breamish changes direction from north-east to north-west as it comes up against the 'wall' of the Fell Sandstone hills and outcrops that stretch in a curved bow shape from Berwick in the north, south to Rothbury and then west to Carter Fell. This takes the river below the steep-sided Harehope Hill and Bewick Hill with, behind them and stretching away, the vast heath and rough grassland of Bewick Moor. The high ground above Old Bewick hamlet is dotted with ancient settlements, forts, cairns, a Bronze Age cist (Blawearie), homesteads, field systems, caves and cup and ring-marked rocks. To take one prominent example, on the top of Bewick Hill is an unusual hill fort (at spot height 232 on the map on p. 78) with two semi-circular enclosures next to each other and with their open sides facing the cliff edge. Behind both of them is another rampart. The west fort contained several hut circles and the east fort contained a series of low walls; they date from the Iron Age and perhaps the Roman period.[31]

After New Bewick Bridge, the river curves round until crossed by a footbridge carrying what must be a very old footpath that

The footbridge at Grid Ref. NU07032074. The old track beyond the bridge slopes up to the Eglingham to Chillingham road at a point east of Old Bewick.

links the hamlet of New Bewick with that of Old Bewick. Thereafter, the river has been artificially confined as it flows north-west between flood embankments before turning north and north-east below Bewick Bridge.

Bewick and Old Bewick together formed the village, being part of the manor of Bewick that was given to the monks of St. Alban's Abbey in 1105. In 1825, Eneas Mackenzie described Old Bewick as 'a pleasant village overhanging the eastern bank of the Till, [sic] in a fine open situation, with a most extensive and delightful prospect...'[32] Mackenzie also refers to the ruined chapel (now restored, see p. 83) a little to the north-west of the village. At that time, he says that Old Bewick was owned by W. S. Bruere Esq. (Mr.

Bruere sold Bewick to Addison John Baker Cresswell, High Sheriff of Northumberland in 1829). In a footnote, Mackenzie refers to an essay by the Rev. Anthony Hedley on the etymology of place-names in Northumberland in which he says that:

> Bewick is one of the few Norman appellations in the county; imposed, probably, by the monks of St. Albans, who, with the church at Eglingham, had very early possession of the township, and other lands in the same parish. It is composed of [Norman French] *beau*, fine, pretty, and the Saxon *wick*, in allusion to its happily chosen site.[33]

However, a more recent interpretation of 'Bewick' suggests that it derives from Anglo-Saxon times and OE for 'bee farm' reflecting the importance of beeswax and particularly honey which was used as a sweetener before the use of sugar.[34] The village must have been there in Anglo-Saxon times because there is an Anglo-Saxon cross built into the church wall. In medieval times, there was a tower in the centre of Old Bewick, first mentioned in 1509 that must have been a defence against the Scots and the Border Reivers.

The Abstract of Education Returns for 1833 show that in Old Bewick (pop. 227) there was:

> One Daily School, wherein are 40 children of both sexes; of these, 10 are paid for by the proprietor of the township, and the remainder by their parents; the master is also allowed a house and garden'.[35]

Whereas in medieval times, the village must have been a bustling village with its own market granted by a charter of Henry III in 1253, the village is now quiet, consisting of only a few cottages.

Old Berwick has a hidden gem—Holy Trinity Church which is up a narrow road alongside the Kirk Burn, a short distance from the hamlet; alternatively, there is a footpath around the lower flank of Bewick Hill which would have been the original route linking the village with the church. The oldest part of the church is 12th century although it is said that the lower part of the building is Saxon. When my companion and I visited the church, we were struck by the size of the building stones. Perhaps the mason was also employed on Northumbrian castle contracts. It is a Grade I listed building.

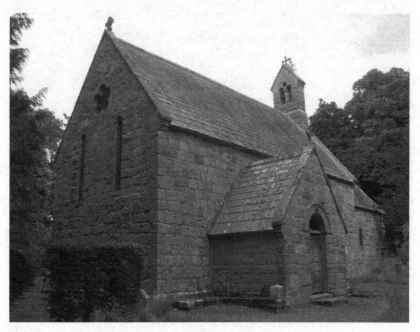

Holy Trinity Church, Old Bewick, from the south-west.

The church is thought to have been damaged by the Scots in the late 13th century. It was restored in the 14th century and then again in the 17th century after damage by the Scottish General Lesley's troops. In the 18th century, the roof was blown off and the building remained a ruin until it was restored and re-roofed in 1866 by Mr. J. C. Langlands, whose monument stands on the corner of the lane. John Langlands was born into a family business making fine silverware in Newcastle but he changed course and became a farmer in Old Bewick where he was renowned and commended for his treatment of employees. He was the discoverer of rock-art on the slopes of Bewick Hill. Later restoration of the church took place in the 19th century.

The clapper bridge across the Kirk Burn, Old Bewick.

The chancel and rose windows in the church commemorate John Langland's wife who died in 1852 and a son killed in New Zealand in 1864. There are many historic features within the church, Norman arches and windows, 14th century effigies, a small belfry bell dating from 1483 and an unusual decorated capital in the chancel. There is much to see in the churchyard, a sundial finial from 1742, memorials, headstones and an old clapper bridge on the route of the ancient track to the village over the Kirk Burn. The word 'clapper' comes from the Anglo-Saxon *cleaca*, 'to bridge stepping stones'.

At the first road junction after the turning to the church, going towards Bewick Bridge, there are the remains of a stone cross that marked the site of the Bewick market. The remains were found in a field near the church in 1874 and the cross was re-erected in the same year in memory of J. C. Langlands.[36]

The R. Breamish flows past the Harehope Estate sawmill on its eastern bank, next to Sawmill and Riverside Cottages and then flows beneath Bewick Bridge.

Sawmill and Riverside Cottages and Bewick Bridge.

4

Bewick Bridge to Chatton Bridge

At Bewick Bridge, Grid Ref. NU05702239, the R. Breamish changes it name to the R. Till. The origin of 'Till' is uncertain. It may be of late 17th century of unknown origin, or the name may come from Scots meaning 'shale' which might relate to glacial deposits brought down by the river. Another source suggests that it comes from a Celtic river name meaning 'to dissolve'. Shaw's Galic [sic] and English Dictionary of 1780 gives *tinim* meaning 'to thaw, dissolve' and *tillam* and *tilladh* meaning 'to turn' and 'a returning'.[1] Eneas Mackenzie associates the change of name from 'Breamish' to 'Till' with a change from a mountainous character to a more gentle course with 'Till' meaning 'a valley'.[2] However, it might just be to do with the tillage or cultivation of land. Or, it might be none of these.

The reason why the change of name occurred at this point may be for the reason suggested in a passing reference by Dr. N. D. Mackichan within an article for The Aln and Breamish Local History Society.[3] Here, he suggests that it may be to do with an administrative boundary going back as far as the Iron Age when he believes there is clear evidence of administrative organization. Presumably, the administrative boundary would have coincided with a divide between groups of people caused by differing geology leading in turn to different agricultural practices. However, the author believes that the obscurity of the idea makes it too difficult to reach a conclusion.

(The Old) Bewick Bridge is an attractive, narrow, hump-backed, sandstone bridge which is listed Grade II. Tony Dickens guessed that it was built in the early 18th century but the listing record puts it at the early 19th century. Dickens refers to a record in Latimer's book of local records for March 29th 1854 relating to the laying of a foundation stone for a suspension bridge at Bewick by Mr. O. B. Cresswell. However it is not clear where this was; there is now no suspension bridge at Bewick—it is unlikely to have preceded the bridge at Old Bewick but perhaps it was a forerunner of the New Berwick Bridge. This is only speculation.[4]

Bewick Bridge from the east, downstream side.

The bridge has a single span with a wide, slightly recessed arch giving a slim appearance. The thin parapets are plain and splay out at either end of the bridge where occasional traffic waits to cross over. Tony Dickens noted an unusual feature with one of the abutments resting on a timber platform, probably of charred oak and the other abutment resting on freestone (sandstone). I was unable to confirm this from my inspection.

Beyond the bridge, the R. Till starts to swing round towards the north-west, passing by woodlands and hillsides with the interesting names of Ravenshole and Folly Banks (to the east and north-east of which are Bewick Folly Farm, Follyburn Wood and Folly Wood). The name 'Ravenshole' must derive from the time when ravens, the largest members of the crow family, were a common sight in Northumberland.

In more recent times, ravens were persecuted in the mistaken belief that they took livestock and game rather than carrion, which is their true diet. Their habitat became confined to upland areas and their numbers were depleted but their fortunes have now improved and they are even to be seen in eastern, low-lying counties of England.

The river passes through marsh and wetland areas, sometimes with flood embankments. The minor road from Bewick Bridge now turns away from the river and rises up to the hamlet of East Lilburn. In 1825, Eneas Mackenzie describes East Lilburn as lying:

> about one mile south-east of West Lilburn, and belongs to Addison John Cresswell Baker, Esq. of Cresswell. It consists of one farmhold and twelve cottages. The proprietor, in 1822, built here one of the most handsome and commodious farm-

houses in the country, and which includes every accommodation for a shooting party.[5]

He also suggests that 'Lill-Burn' (sic) is derived from the Danish, *lille*, meaning 'little' and mentions that *lile* is still used for 'little' in Cumberland and Westmoreland. The Lilburn Burn, which rises within the Northumberland National Park in Ilderton Parish, joins the Till at East Lilburn. There is the site of a medieval village at East Lilburn.

In this book, my occasional deviations from the route do not include the many tributaries of the Breamish and Till. The Lilburn Burn is no exception but it is worth mentioning that the Secretary of State was notified in 1999 of areas of relict juniper woodland, *Juniperes communis* and alder woodland, *Alnus glutinosa*, in specified areas within the SSSI, along the upper reaches of the Lilburn Burn on the eastern edge of the Northumberland National Park. The notification was because juniper is rare in Northumberland and alder has a restricted distribution.[6]

The Roddam Burn also joins the R. Till near East Lilburn. Again, the wooded Roddam Dene, west of the A697 road, is not on my route but I am mentioning it because it is of interest to geologists as it is the site of the nationally important Roddam Dene Conglomerate, the most exposed of the coarse conglomerate outcrops along the flanks of the Cheviot Hills. It comprises a mix of beds of reddish conglomerates of pebble to boulder size, sandstone, shale, mudstone and marls forming part of the early Carboniferous, Inverclyde Group and within what is known as the Kinnesswood Formation named after Kinneswood near Loch Leven, Fife, in Scotland .[7]

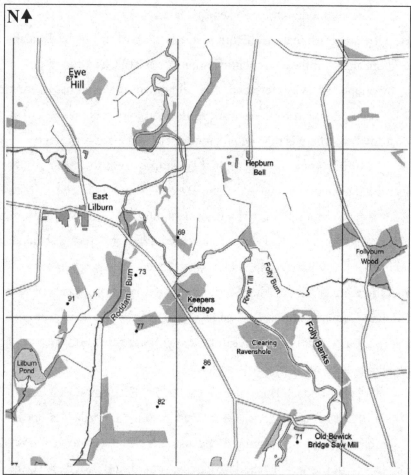

The R. Till north of Old Bewick Bridge, flowing past East Lilburn where it is joined by the Lilburn Burn and the Roddam Burn. 1 sq.km. grids. Contains Ordnance Survey data © Crown copyright and database right 2014.

Ewe Hill, shown on the map above (at the spot height of 87 m.) is on the line of the ancient Devil's Causeway. On the western side of the hill is a Bronze Age standing stone with cup and ring marks.[8] Nearby is a WWII pillbox; I have mentioned one before near Hedgeley Bridge but this one is on a 'stop line' of 26 pillboxes between Wooler and Alnwick, probably built in 1940. There was another 'stop line' between Wooler and Belford but there were many other pillboxes along the coast and inland.[9]

The R. Till flows below Chillingham Newtown Bridge at Grid Ref. NU04932515. The bridge is a scheduled ancient monument but does not appear to have a listing grade. Tony Dickens dates it to 1859 and gives the span of the single arch, stone bridge as 60 ft. 9 ins. with an arch height of 18 ft. 9 ins., parapets of 4 ft.1 ins. and a width between parapets of 12 ft. $2^{1}/_{2}$ ins.[10] It is an attractive, sandstone bridge with squared blocks built to courses and a fine segmental arch. There is a pier with a low cap at the centre of the parapet walls and these walls slope down to the wing walls. The bridge carries the western approach road to Chillingham Castle from Newtown.

Chillingham Newtown Bridge from the south-west.

The status of the road is clearly demonstrated on the east side of the bridge, rising through an avenue to the West Lodge of the castle on the Chatton road. In 1868, Newtown was described in the *National Gazetteer of Great Britain and Ireland* as 'a township in the parish of Chillingham...Near the village is Hurlstone-cross, 12 feet in height, the soil is of a clayey nature, with a subsoil of rock and limestone'.[11]

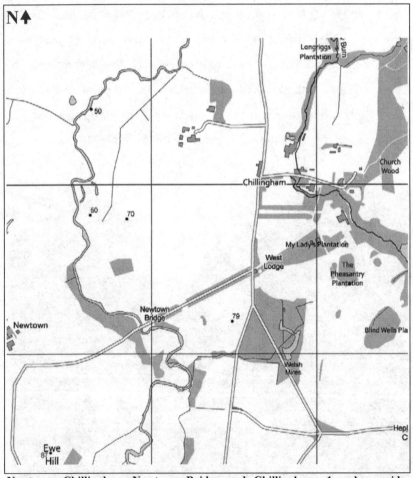

Newtown, Chillingham Newtown Bridge and Chillingham. 1 sq.km. grids. Contains Ordnance Survey data © Crown copyright and database right 2014.

The Hurlstone-cross is now known as the 'Hurl Stone' which stands in a field south-west of Newtown. It is about 12 feet high with a chunk out of the top, perhaps caused by a lightning strike. It is thought to be early medieval (410-1066 AD) and may have been a boundary stone, a road marker or the remains of a cross. It may also have been moved to its present position from somewhere else. It is on private land and therefore not accessible to the public. Nearby is a three-storey castellated folly built by the Lilburn Estate to commemorate the millennium in 2000.

In 1866, George Tate writes that a favourite haunt of fairies was 'the Hurle Stane near to Chillingham New Town, around which they danced to the sound of elfin music, singing,

> "Wind about and turn again
> And thrice around the Hurle Stane;
> Round about and wind again
> And thrice around the Hurle Stane."'[12]

Unfortunately, the fairy singing did not float across the field to my roadside vantage point when I was there.

At Newtown, there is the site of a Romano-British settlement, a medieval village and a tower. In 1542, Sir Robert Bowes and Sir Rauffe Ellerker spoke of the deficiences of the tower (owner Will'm Strouther) during their survey of the East and Middle Marches:

> At Est Newton there ys a lytle towre and a stone house joined to the same the walls of which stone house ys so lowe that in the last warres the Scotts wan the same stone house & sett fyre on yt and had tyhereby almost burnte the tower and all. The experience whereof sheweth that yt were expedyente to

rase the walls of the said stone house and to fortefye the same able for the defence of common skyrmyshes...[13]

At Chillingham and Hepburn, there is also evidence suggesting the existence of medieval villages; these may have been removed or relocated because of expansion of the Chillingham estate or, as with many medieval villages, they may have declined because of pestilent disease or changes to farming practices.[14]

It is worth straying from the route again in order to see the bastle at Hepburn and the view from the hillfort of Ros Castle.

Hepburn Bastle is on a rise overlooking the Till valley. It was previously overgrown with ivy but is now clear.

Hepburn or Hebburn Bastle is a medieval building of the early 16th century that was modified and added to before being abandoned in the 18th century; it is a Grade II* listed building. In

1896, Sir James Mackenzie gave a succinct description of the ruined tower as:

> a large oblong block, a "bastle" or bastille house, with a vaulted basement and a dungeon. It is two storeys high above the entrance, with gables at the E. and W. ends, and the windows are good.[15]

Bastles were fortified houses, not as large as a castle or as tall as a pele tower, built throughout the dangerous border areas for family protection against Scots or English raids. Hepburn was owned by Nicholas de Hebburn in 1271 and the Hebburns owned the land down to 1588 when there was an arbitration as a result of a blood feud with the Story family following the murder of a John Story. The Hebburns retained ownership until the 18th century when an heiress married 'a clerical adventurer' named Brudenell after which it was sold to the Earl of Tankerville in about 1770.[16]

The bastle was certainly in existence and in reasonable order in 1542 when inspected by Sir Robert Bowes and Sir Rauffe Ellerker, 'At Hebburne ys a lytle toure of thinerytaunce of Thomas Hebburne in reasonable good rep'ac'ons.'[17] In 1891, Cadwaller John Bates raised a query on whether this was the same bastle because of its description as 'lytle' and wondered whether 'a heap of stones near the park wall' was the original site. However, he thought that Sir Robert and Sir Rauffe would have mentioned a nearby 'strong house' if it had been there. Bates mentions the first reference to the building by Bowes and Ellerker at which time it was 'owned and inhabited by Thomas Hebburn when it was supposed to be capable of accommodating a garrison of twenty horsemen'.[18]

Ros Castle at Grid Ref. NU08112532 is well worth the climb from the roadside at Hepburn Moor (or, for a better walk, from the car park at Hepburn Quarry) to its summit at 315 m. (1,033 ft.). It is possible to see seven castles from here, Lindisfarne, Bamburgh, Dunstanburgh, Warkworth, Alnwick, Ford and Chillingham. Looking west, there is a magnificent view over Chillingham Castle and Park across the Till valley to Wooler, Yeavering Bell and other northern summits of the Cheviot Hills. This was not the site of a castle but of a defended Iron Age settlement, surrounded then by an earth and stone bank and a ditch, with hut circles inside. There is another Iron Age fort to the west, above Hepburn Crags.[19] The name, 'Ros' probably comes from the Brythonic, *rhos*, meaning a promontory, moor, waste or high land.[20]

The view looking north-west over Chillingham Park from Ros Castle

The archaeological features are difficult to see because of the thick heather that covers the summit and the Chillingham boundary wall that cuts across it. A small stone platform built into the east side of the wall has been suggested as the site of a medieval or post-medieval beacon but it is now used as a viewing point with topographs built into its sides. There is also a plaque on the trig. point to say that Ros Castle Camp was a favourite resort of Sir Edward Grey, afterwards Viscount Grey of Falloden, Foreign Secretary, December 1905 to December 1916. The plaque also records that the camp was presented to the National Trust in 1936 as part of a national memorial to Viscount Grey. When I was there on a bright but cold, November day, there was an active and far from hibernating ladybird striding across the trig. point.

Chillingham Castle was the seat of the linked Grey and Bennet families from the 15th century until the 1980s. The castle fell into serious disrepair before it was purchased and restored by Sir Humphry Wakefield whose wife is descended from a branch of the Grey family. John Grey (1384-1421) was granted the title 1st Earl of Tankerville (and Comté of Tancarville in Normandy) by Henry V for his service in the Hundred Years War. His father was Thomas Grey of Heaton, a castle further down the R. Till. The earldom was forfeited during the Wars of the Roses in the 15th century and the lands in Normandy were lost in 1453. The title was re-created in the 17th century and again in the 18th century and the present holder still has the name Grey-Bennet. However, the last Earl of Tankerville to live at Chillingham was the 6th Earl who died there in 1899. Mawer believed that 'Chillingham' meant 'Home of Ceofel or of his sons'.[21]

Eneas Mackenzie, writing in 1825, said that the castle:

Stands on a fine eminence, surrounded by trees, at a short distance from the church. It is a square heavy structure, of four storeys in the wings and three in the centre, and is of the order of architecture used in the reign of queen [sic] Elizabeth. From the centre area a flight of steps lead into a balustrade, ornamented with the effigies of British warriors armed, cut in stone. The apartments are awkward and small, and the communications irregular. Here are several good portraits, a full length of lord chancellor Bacon, another of lord treasurer Burleigh; a gaudy painting of Buckingham, in a white satin gilded vest, gold and white striped breeches, effeminate and fantastical; a good portrait of king Charles; a picture of James II of the most unhappy countenance.[22]

Mackenzie's description of Chillingham Castle is shorter than his description of a large, live frog discovered in a sealed off cavity behind a marble fireplace that was being removed from one of the apartments. How did it get there? Was the cement soft when it went in and how did it survive without food, light, company and only 'the dews that might pass through the texture of marble'? According to William Hutchinson the 18th century historian, 'if the toad was as large as represented (in a painting), it was wonderful indeed, for size as well as its existence, being near as big as a hat crown'.[23]

Bowes and Ellerker found the castle to be in good shape in 1542; it had to be really, as Sir Robert Ellerker was the custodian:

The Castell of Chyllingham of thinheritaunce of yonge Rauffe Graye of the same beinge in the kinges Ma[te] warde &

order duringe his mynorytie & none age ys in measurable good repac'ons for S^r. Robt Ellerker knighte havynge the custodye & gov'nance of the said castell hath of late newly rep'elled the same.[24]

A few minutes walk from the castle is St. Peter's Church which is on the site of a 12th century church and retains some Norman stonework. The pews are 19th century and the sanctuary was refurbished in 1967. There is a magnificent, intricately carved tomb of Sir Ralph Grey (1406-1443) and his wife, Elizabeth, with their alabaster effigies and some surviving paintwork, carved in 1440. Sir Ralph was the nephew of Sir John Grey, 1st Earl of Tankerville; Sir Ralph captured Roxburgh Castle in Scotland with 81 men and held it against the Scots for eight days until English reinforcements arrived. He and his son fought on opposite sides during the Wars of the Roses and Sir Ralph condemned his son to death by being hanged, drawn and quartered, a sentence that was reduced to beheading.

Chillingham Park is home to the herd of white cattle that have lived there for 800 years. The cattle are said to be the only survivors of wild herds that used to roam Britain's forests. The cattle are owned by the Chillingham Wild Cattle Association set up by the 8th Earl of Tankerville, his widow and their son. The Park is now also in the ownership of the Association.

Mackenzie mentions John Bailey, the Chillingham estate steward who, in the late 1770s, laid out the Park as a designed landscape by clearing away the old features and creating large areas of pasture interspersed with new oak and beech trees. John Bailey was also responsible for improving the design of the horse-drawn plough as set out in his *An Essay on the Construction of the Plough, deduced from Mathematical Principles* and described in detail by James Donaldson in his *Modern Agriculture or the Present State of Husbandry in Great Britain* in 1796.[25] For example, Bailey determined what proportion the breadth of the plough should bear to the depth so as to expose the greatest surface, as calculated by mathematical formulae. Bailey's talents went beyond this— Mackenzie tells how he 'formed a new era in rural improvements' and 'that of irrigation merits peculiar notice' as in the following instance:

> In the vicinity of Wooler there is a large tract of low flat ground (called haughs) adjoining the rivers Till and Glen, which was frequently overflown. Mr. Bailey made the attempt to embank them at Yevering [sic] in the year 1787; which answering the purpose, the practice was soon after adopted on the haughs of Turvilaws, Doddington, Ewart, &c. by which the lands were more than doubled in value.

As a result of this 'he was most extensively employed to survey and value estates in the north of England'.[26]

Earlier, I mentioned the small hamlet of East Lilburn. To the west of Newtown and about two miles south-west of the entrance to Chillingham Castle is that part of Lilburn to the north of the Lilburn Burn, the area that appears on the modern OS map as 'Lilburn Tower, Observatory, chapel (remains of) Lilburn Tower (rems. of), Castle Hill, Earthwork, Lilburntower Farm, Gamekeeper's House' and, if extended to the north, 'Lilburn Hill' and West Lilburn House'. This was once known as West Lilburn. In 1825, Eneas Mackenzie describes West Lilburn as being 'pleasantly seated on a rising ground east from the Coldstream road'. He tells us that it was a town and lordship belonging to the barony of Wark held by Robert de Ros whose son, Robert, defected to the Scots and forfeited his estates. The lordship was held by the Lilburns from the time of King Edward II onwards with the family being active in battles and politics. Amongst the many family stories, Sir John Lilburn was captured by the Scots at Carham in 1370 (not to be confused with the Battle of Carham in 1016 or 1018) and at the Battle of Otterburn in 1388 and Sir Thomas Lilburn was the representative in Parliament for Northumberland. The property passed to the Clennel family and, eventually to Henry Collingwood, nephew of Thomas Clennel. Mackenzie says:

> Henry Collingwood, Esq. of Lilburn, was high sheriff of Northumberland in the year 1793. At the west end of the village, enclosed with trees, are the ruins of the ancient tower and mansion of the Lilburns. The remains of a chapel may also be traced. At the east end stands Lilburn Tower, which is a neat modern building, and the seat of Henry Collingwood, Esq. one of the remaining branches of the ancient Northumbrian family of the Collingwoods.[27]

Henry's son, John (brother of Admiral, later Lord, Cuthbert Collingwood who was second in command at the Battle of Trafalgar) demolished the existing house and commissioned the architect John Dobson of Newcastle to design the new house that was started in 1828 and finished in 1848. The estate remained in the Collingwood family into the 20th century and the estate is now privately owned as part of Lilburn Estates Farming Partnership which includes agricultural holdings across Glendale and the north of the county.

Lilburn Tower is not open to the public. The ruins of the original 15th century manor house and its pele tower (West Lilburn Tower) are listed Grade II* and the old chapel is Grade II. Castle Hill is an Iron Age fort that was surrounded by circular ramparts. Part of the site has been destroyed leaving about one quarter of the ramparts visible.[28]

Lilburn Tower glimpsed through the trees from the public road.

Just south-west of Lilburn Tower is an astronomical observatory built in about 1852 by Edward Collingwood and equipped with a $6\frac{1}{3}$ ins. Troughton & Simms telescope and a 4 ins. transit telescope. Edward Collingwood went blind soon after completion and so the observatory was never used. It received some refurbishment in the 1990s but it remains in its original condition as a 'time capsule' (no public access). It is listed Grade II*.[29]

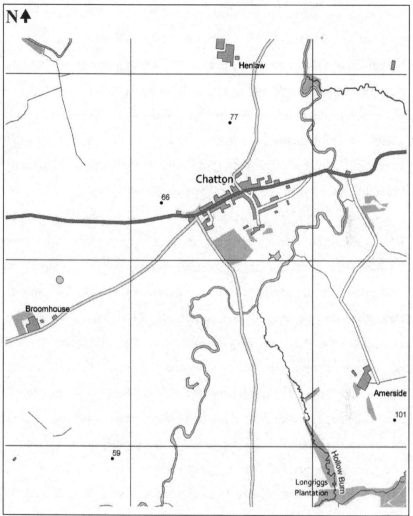

R. Till flows under Chatton Iron Bridge and Chatton Bridge. 1 sq.km. grids. Contains Ordnance Survey data © Crown copyright and database right 2014.

    The R. Till continues its meandering course north-north-east from Chillingham, first of all passing to the west of Chillingham Barns farm and then onwards towards Chatton Iron Bridge. The farm is the cluster of buildings in the middle top grid of the previous map on p. 92. This area, as well as Chillingham Park to the east, is studded with disused quarries. In the wood at Chillingham Barns, there are the sites of a tile works, kiln and clay pit, probably used for the manufacture of drainage pipes in the 19th century when low-lying land was being improved for agricultural improvement.[30] Chillingham Barns Farm was the home of Sir Jacob Wilson (1836-1905), the land agent for Chillingham Estates from 1881. He was appointed Knight Commander of the Royal Victorian Order in 1889 and was Honorary Director of the Royal Agricultural Society.[31]

The meandering course of the river has produced an oxbow lake that can be seen on the map on p. 103; this shows where the course of the river has moved laterally across the flood plain in the past caused by differences in erosion between the shallower, slower, inner edge and the deeper, faster, outer edge of the meander. Material is eroded from the outer edges and deposited on the inner edges A meander loop becomes exaggerated and the 'neck' of the meander becomes narrower until such time as the river takes the shorter course across the neck, perhaps when in spate, leaving the loop isolated as an oxbow lake. Oxbow lakes are typical of the middle and lower course of a river where vertical erosion is replaced by lateral erosion.

A skull dating to the Roman era was found at a spot on the side of the large loop to the west of Chatton Iron Bridge in the middle of the map on p. 103. No other remains were found and the find remains a mystery.[32]

Chatton Iron Bridge was described by Tony Dickens in 1975 as 'a rather hideous and insignificant bridge…It is a lattice girder type bridge with metal cross girders with the main lattice girders forming

Chatton Iron Bridge from the west. Grid Ref. NU05602771

R. Till looking west from Chatton Iron Bridge.

the parapets, which have a height of 5 feet 4 inches. It has a span of 56 feet and a width of 20 feet.'[33] When I was there, the bridge reminded me of an army Bailey bridge that had been long forgotten and it was certainly in need of some repainting. It rests on two substantial stone piers that were probably part of an older bridge. Tony Dickens mentions a note written by Archdeacon Singleton (Archdeacon of Northumberland 1826-1842):

> There is a fearful ford between Chatton and Chillingham which I crossed. Lord Tankerville told me he had engaged to build a bridge there'.[34]

This bridge may have been the forerunner of the present iron bridge.

The R. Till is joined by the Hollow Burn before passing to the south east of Chatton village and beneath the very attractive Chatton Bridge, listed Grade II. English Heritage describes it as being;

> early 18th century and late 19th century possibly with older core. Ashlar and rock-faced ashlar. North side is oldest. 2 broad segmental arches with smaller segmental flood arch to left. 2 triangular cut-waters carried up to parapet to make indents for pedestrians. Cut-waters between 2 main arches more pronounced than between left and flood arches. Plain parapet and approach walls. Older masonry on right approach and abutment with indication of steeper, earlier roadway, Bridge doubled in width in late 19th century. Rock-faced façade and rusticated vaults. 4 stone steps down from east of north side.[35]

The bridge carries the B6348 road from Wooler, through Chatton village and eastwards to join the A1 road, south of Belford.

Chatton Bridge, south face.

From the bridge at Grid Ref. NU06092848, the B6348 runs west into the attractive village of Chatton described by Archbishop Singleton as 'a long village and the houses covered with red tiles, but this is an improvement on the old heather roofs, whatever the lovers of the picturesque may say'.[36] The name 'Chatton', according to Mawer, derives from 'Farm of Cetta or Ceatta'.[37] In 1825, Eneas Mackenzie describes the parish of Chatton, bounded by the parishes of Lowick, Doddington, Wooler, Eglingham, Chillingham, Bambrough and Belford, having '274 houses and 1460 inhabitants; also two schools, attended by about 120 children, and a Sunday-school, which is in a declining state'. He mentions lime-works in the north and east of the parish carried on by J. A. Wilkie, Esq. of Hetton and J. Pratt, Esq. of Bellshill. There was also one of the largest annual fairs in the north, held on Whitsun-Tuesday, for cattle, horses and sheep and for the hiring of servants.[38]

Chatton village was the largest in the parish with upwards of 70 families. The Duke of Northumberland was the patron and the church, dedicated to the Holy Cross, was 'a vicarage, valued in the king's books at £12, 10s. 0½d.' Mackenzie mentions that the church was built in 1763 and contains French Colours captured by 'the son of the present vicar', Lt. Samuel Cook of HMS *Swallow*.

There was also the resting place, without tombstone, of Mr. John Dial, an eminent mathematics teacher at Bamburgh Castle 'whose jovial disposition and fondness for company led him into irregularities…decidedly incompatible with the ideas which his employers entertained of the necessity of strict morals and good example'. Because of his 'improper habits' he lost his job and ended up 'in very indigent circumstances'. A sorry tale and, unfortunately, one often repeated since then.[39]

The manor of Chatton belonged to the Vescy family, was sold to the Percys, was forfeited to the Crown and was then bestowed on George Duke of Clarence by his brother, Edward IV.[40] According to William Whelan, in 1856, the village was the property of the Duke of Northumberland who was also Lord of the Manor and patron of the church. However, the living, in the archdeaconry of Lindisfarne and the deanery of Norham, seems to have reduced a little to £12, 6s. 0½d.

The construction of the church in 1763 is preceded by the commencement of the parish register in 1715.[41] This fits in with the creation of the parish in 1712 to serve the communities of Chatton, Fowberry, Hazelrig, Hetton, Hetton House, Horton, Lynham and Weetwood. But there must have been a much earlier building because

Whelan recounts an interesting story about the sexton's discovery of a stone coffin when he was digging a grave on the north side of the church in 1814. Inside were human remains weighted down with three stones. The skull was 'almost perfect, but nearly full of water, and the teeth of the upper jaw were a full set; the thigh bone measured eighteen inches'. A silver penny of Robert the Bruce was found with a steel spur and pieces of brass and ironwork, probably from a helmet.

The then vicar of Chatton, the Rev. Joseph Cook of Newton Hall, suggested that, in 1318, as Robert the Bruce had been excommunicated by the Pope for 'contumacy' (refusal to obey authority) to the Pope's messengers and had captured the castles of Berwick, Wark, Harbottle and Mitford and laid waste all the surrounding lands, it is possible that one of his knights was killed or died here and, as a follower of an excommunicated king, was buried on the north side of the church in ground 'for the unhallowed interment of excommunicated unfortunates'.[42]

Chatton had two fortified towers in medieval times, the first being at Grieve's Law to the north of the village which had been built by 1415 but is not mentioned after 1616 and the second, known as the 'Vicar's Pele', which had also been built by 1415 and is now below the 19th century vicarage at the end of Church Hill Road. No remains survive from either tower. Part of the present village overlies a medieval settlement. Traces of this were excavated at Mill Hill in 1999 before houses were built on the site. Earthworks, ditches, traces of 18th century buildings, pits and 13th century pottery were found.[43]

At the end of the 19th century, the village was a bustling place with many trades represented, such as a mason, a carpenter, an undertaker, a blacksmith and a tailor. There were two churches, a school, a post office, a reading room, a brewery and a number of shops. Today, the village is quieter and is designated as a Conservation Area but there is still a thriving community with a church, a first school, an hotel, a village shop and an art gallery. A Millenium sculpture in the shape of the village streets stands proudly at the eastern edge of the village.

Further to the east and over the bridge is Chatton Park House, a Grade II listed building built between 1830-1840, now a grand Bed and Breakfast establishment but, at one time, the home of the Dukes of Northumberland. It seems that Chatton Park was enclosed towards the end of the 13th century and, in the 17th century, was the subject of a dispute between the inhabitants of Chattan and Sir Ralph Grey who was accused of enclosing land at Chatton Common into Chillingham Park.[44] It is often not appreciated that land clearances (of tenants) were taking place in England long before the more widely known Highland Clearances. Because of the increasing profits to be made from sheep in the 16th century, landowners were turning land over to sheep production but also enclosing areas of their estates, well before the Enclosure Acts of the 18th and 19th centuries. Eric Kerridge tells us that, in 1567, 'the 11 husbandmen, 8 cottagers, 4 cottiers and 1 smith of Tuggal had recently been reduced to 8 farmers'. Also, 'About this date, Sir Thomas Gray [sic] of Chillingham is reported to have expelled 340 men, women and children from Newham in one day'.[45]

Chatton Park and Chatton Park Farm flank the Mill Burn which flows into the Till north of the village. There were once two mills along the burn and, on the other side of the road from Chatton

Park Farm is the site of the Chatton tile works that had a clay pit and kilns, one of which survives in modified form. To the north-east of Chatton Park Hill were lime works and there used to be a windmill that might have been associated with the lime works.[46] Nearby was Chatton Colliery and there were scattered quarries and coal workings. Chatton Colliery was owned by Chatton Coal & Lime Co., then Joseph Henderson and, finally, R. Brown, from the 1880s until its closure in 1903.[47]

Looking south-east from Chatton Bridge along the R. Till towards Birley Hill and Amersidelaw Plantation.

5

Chatton Bridge to Doddington Bridge

Frrom Chatton Bridge, the R. Till heads north, being joined by the Mill Burn from the east until, at the point where it is joined by the Allery or Lyham Burn from the east, the lie of the land causes it to swing sharply to the west and then take an extraordinary course through all 360 degrees of the compass as far as Fowberry Bridge.

R. Till looking north from Chatton Bridge with Park Plantation distant, right.

CHATTON BRIDGE TO DODDINGTON BRIDGE

On the east side of the river, the land rises gently and then steeply to Park Plantation, above which is the summit of Chatton Park Hill. Here are some of the finest examples of cup and ring rock-art in Northumberland, probably from Bronze Age or Neolithic times. There is also an Iron Age fort (Chatton Law camp) surrounded by two ramparts and another Iron Age or Roman settlement with hut circles and possibly a livestock enclosure.[1]

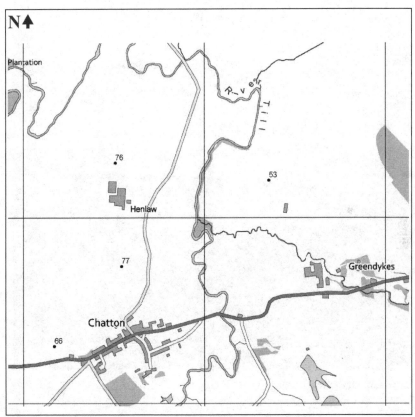

The R. Till between Chatton and Lyham Bridge. The Mill Burn is seen entering opposite Henlaw. The Allery or Lyham Burn enters where it says 'River Till' at top right. Plant Plantation on the slopes of Chatton Park Hill is where the grey 'finger' appears on the right of the map. 1 sq.km. grids. Contains Ordnance Survey data © Crown copyright and database right 2014.

On the west side of the river is the Chatton sewage works and, on the west side of the road to West Lyham, is Henlaw Farm. South of West Lyham, the river passes beneath Lyham Bridge at Grid Ref. NU05882983. Lyham was, at one time a manor which must have encompassed the present hamlets of North Lyham, South Lyham, Old Lyham and West Lyham with land at Lyham Hill and Lyham Moor, the source of the Allery or Lyham Burn. The manor was possessed by the de Lyham family from the 13th century and it passed to the del Strother family by marriage in the 14th century.

Lyham Bridge from the south-west.

Tony Dickens described Lyham Bridge in 1975 as 'a lattice girder bridge...not particularly attractive although it does rest on ashlar masonry abutments which originally may have formed part of

114

an older bridge…'.[2] He puts the date at 1890 and the dimensions as being, span 54 feet, height of parapets 6 feet at the mid span and width between parapets of 12 feet. Nothing seems to have changed since 1975 except that the colour of the girders is now a strange shade of lilac.

From here, the river snakes westward passing the Labour in Vain Plantation (not the only one in the area—there is another at Chillingham) and Dickey Island Plantation and around the south side of Hetton House.

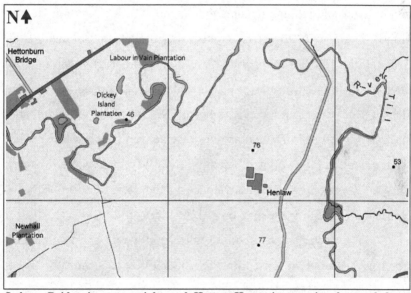

Lyham Bridge is at top right and Hetton House is opposite the road from Hettonburn Bridge. 1 sq.km. grids. Contains Ordnance Survey data © Crown copyright and database right 2014.

In 1825, Eneas Mackenzie wrote:

Hetton is a small village situate on the north side of the Till, about one mile north-west from Chatton. At some distance

northward is *Hetton Hall*, the pleasant seat of John Allen
Wilkie, Esq.[3]

Hetton Hall is not to be confused with Hetton House. The former is an
impressive Grade II* listed, privately owned, 15th century tower house
with 18th and 19th century additions. Mackenzie's 'one mile' is one
mile north of the parish boundary whereas the Hall is over three miles
north of Chatton village on a tributary of the Till, the Hetton Burn.

Hetton House is a private house, the gardens of which
overlook the Till. It is also Grade II* listed, being an attractive mid-
18th century house with an older core, a 19th century range to the right
and exterior and interior features that support the high listing. Hetton
House, along with Fowberry Tower, was used as a Voluntary Aid
hospital (the 12th Northumberland VA Hospital) during WWI, to look
after convalescing soldiers. VA hospitals were organised by the
British Red Cross and the Knights of St. John of Jerusalem and
staffed by V.A.D.'s (Voluntary Aid Detachments) of women who
were trained in First Aid and Nursing.[4] In WWII, there was a Prisoner
of War camp opposite Hetton House to the west of where it says
Hettonburn Bridge in the map on p. 115.[5]

The river now swings north-northwest to pass under
Fowberry Bridge at Grid Ref. NU05882983, a Grade II listed
structure which Tony Dickens describes as:

> A most graceful structure, with two masonry arches, the main
> one spanning the Till has a span of 59 feet and the smaller
> arch, which is really a flood arch, spans the drive leading to
> Fowberry Tower and measures just over 10 feet. The arches
> have a breadth of 14 feet 7 inches. It is a hog backed

bridge...constructed of ashlar masonry...The bridge was probably constructed in 1769...[6]

Fowberry Bridge from the south.

The track to Fowberry Tower can just be seen in the photograph, heading south from the flood arch. Mawer gives many depictions of the name from the 13th and 14th centuries. The two earliest are *Folebir* from c. 1250 and *Follebiri* from 1288 which Mawer says derive from OE, *folan byrig* meaning 'foals' *burh*', or where foals are bred although *burh* may refer to a fortified place.[7] Fowberry Tower, a Grade II* listed building, was originally a fortified house dating from at least the 16th century but it was rebuilt in the 18th century. In 1825, Eneas Mackenzie says that the Tower was the seat of William de Folebyr who 'held Folebyr, Coldmorton

117

and Hessilrigg by one knight's fee, of the old feoffment of the barony of Vescy'. In 1524, the son and heir of William de Fowberry captured 200 Scots on their return from a plundering operation but, eight years later, the Scots plundered Fowberry. In 1663, it was the property of William Strother of Kirk Newton 'but charged upon "Mr. Heron of Fowberry" in the rental for raising train-bands [local militia]'. In 1825, the property was owned and lived in by Matthew Culley who had bought it from Sir Francis Blake, Bart.[8]

Matthew and George Culley were farming brothers who left their mark on farming practices and the history of agriculture in north Northumberland and beyond. Their father owned and worked a 200 acre estate at Denton in County Durham but the brothers had an ambition to set up on their own, something that was encouraged by their father who sent them to study under a leading stockbreeder in Leicestershire. The brothers started farming at Fenton in Glendale building up to over 1100 acres and then gradually taking on other farms at Crookham Westfield, Eastfield, Barmoor Red House, Wark, Grindon, Thornington, Longknowe and Shotton. Eventually they were working between 3000 and 4000 acres, leased from landowners such as Lord Tankerville, John Orde and the Askews of Pallinsburn. Their farming success enabled them to become landowners and they bought the Akeld estate in 1795, Easington Grange in 1801 and Fowberry in 1807.

Matthew (1731-1804) and George (1735-1813) enclosed and improved land and brought waste land into production. They enriched the soil, improved drainage, introduced new crops and brought in a new rotation system adapted from the four-crop Norfolk rotation

118

system. But they were particularly renowned for their improved methods of livestock breeding such as the introduction of the 'Dishley' breed of sheep or 'New Leicester' from which came the 'Border Leicester' breed.[9] So, with John Bailey's improvements at Chillingham in the late 18th century and the Culleys' advances at Fowberry and elsewhere into the early 19th century, north Northumberland has earned its place in agricultural history.

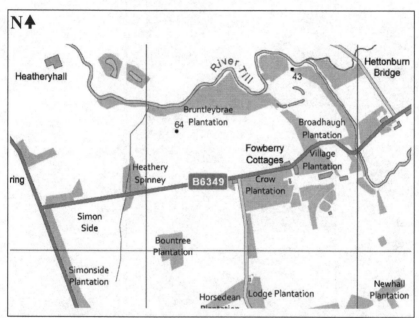

Fowberry Bridge is to the east of Broadhaugh and Village Plantations. 1 sq. km. grids. Contains Ordnance Survey data © Crown copyright and database right 2014.

The course of the R. Till after passing under Fowberry Bridge can be seen on the above map. The Hetton Burn enters the river near spot-height 43 and the Devil's Causeway crosses the river after traversing Tippet Hill, the summit of which is marked by the spot-height 64 on the map. The strength of flow of the Till makes me wonder whether there was a Roman bridge; this seems to be most likely rather than just relying on a ford. Speculation again. North of Heatheryhall, the river loops around to the south of the hamlet of Horton.

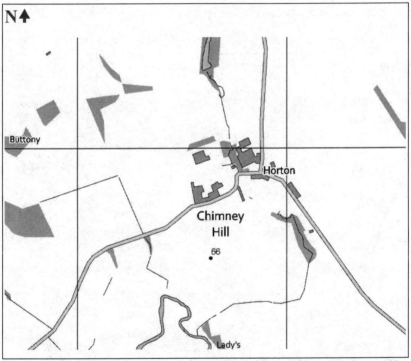

The loop of the river is to the west of Lady's (Plantation). 1 sq.km. grids. Contains Ordnance Survey data © Crown copyright and database right 2014.

Eneas Mackenzie wrote:

Horton stands in a bleak and naked country…Scarcely any remains of the *Castle of Horton* now exist, the venerable ruins having been appropriated to the building or repairing of the out-houses of the adjoining farmers. Horton was held of the barony of William Vescy, by William Tuberville, for half a knight's fee;...[10]

After this, the castle was the seat of a branch of the Greys of Chillingham and, in 1825, was held by Earl Grey of Howick to whom it had devolved on the death of Sir Henry Grey, Bart. Further information records that Horton Castle:

> was first mentioned in a list of castles from 1415. In 1542 it was described as a 'great tower'. By 1715 it was in a ruined state though it was repaired and from 1740 to 1808 it was used as a house. It was finally demolished in the early 19th century. Nothing can be seen on the site today except for a few fragments of worked stone.[11]

There are cup and ring-marked rocks and enclosures and hut circles to the north of the hamlet, on Horton Moor and there is a possibility that, south of Horton, there was a Roman marching camp on the Devil's Causeway which passes to the east of Horton until it coincides with the straight, minor road that runs north to Lowick.

Flowing past Sweet Haugh, the R. Till flows south-west and under Weetwood Bridge at Grid Ref. NU01852946. Above the bridge on the hillside is the Iron Age hillfort of Simonside Camp which has a central enclosure and smaller enclosures attached to it with possible Roman houses overlying part of the site. The deserted medieval village of Clavering lies below and to the east of the fort. No traces of it remain today.[12]

Weetwood Bridge has to be one, but only one, of my favourite bridges over the Breamish and the Till. Chillingham Newtown, Chatton and Fowberry Bridges have all struck a cord with me and there are more to come. Weetwood Bridge has a particularly attractive, open location with good views looking south-west towards the Cheviot Hills. Between Fowberry Bridge and Weetwood Bridge, the Till is funnelled through a gap in the Fell Sandstone escarpment to the east of Wooler and passes beneath the steep slopes of Weetwood Moor giving a dramatic setting for Weetwood Bridge.

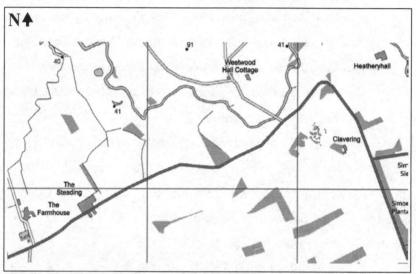

The R. Till flows under Weetwood Bridge, then south-east of Weetwood Hall (under the word 'Cottage') and towards Doddington Bridge. 1 sq.km. grids. Contains Ordnance Survey data © Crown copyright and database right 2014.

Weetwood Bridge is listed Grade I and was built in the 16th century and altered in the mid 18th century. It has pinkish ashlar facings and a wide arch forming a hump-back or hog-back and is flanked by pilasters, each containing inset niches. The north end has square projections with blocked, round-headed arches and round end-piers with conical finials. The parapets are of contrasting, grey ashlar with flat coping-stones. The roadway is narrow but the parapet splays out either side to allow vehicles to pass.[13]

Weetwood Bridge from the south-west.

Weetwood Bridge is on the route of St. Cuthbert's Way, the $62^1/_2$ miles long walking route that starts in Melrose and ends on the Holy Island of Lindisfarne. The route crosses the bridge from south to north on the stage between Wooler and Fenwick and the recent resin-bonded gravel on the bridge footways will certainly stand up to heavy foot traffic. It is said that the Earl of Surrey and the English army crossed the Till in the vicinity of Weetwood in 1513 before moving north past Doddington on their way to Barmoor where they camped on the night before the Battle of Flodden. According to Tony Dickens, at the beginning of the 20th century there used to be a toll-house on the right hand side of the road leading to Whitsun Bank near Wooler, where an old lady took the tolls and also sold 'pop' and Woodbine

123

cigarettes at five for $3^{1}/_{2}$d in pre-decimal currency. Also, until 1880, the Whitsun Fair was held near Weetwood Bridge; this dated back to at least 1595 when Sir John Carey reported that Kerr of Cessford had tried to ambush the Storeys on their way to the fair.[14]

Weetwood (Hall) was described by Eneas Mackenzie in 1825, 'Weetwood, the seat of John Ord [sic], Esq. is most delightfully situate on the north banks of the Till, at a short distance south from Horton Castle'.[15] The Hall is a Grade II listed building described as being late 18th century with 19th century work and with a medieval core. In particular, the interior thick walls would have been part of the former tower house that would have been built as a protection against the Scots.[16] The tower was first mentioned in the mid 16th century but it may date back to the 13th or 14th centuries.[17]

View from Weetwood Bridge towards Humbleton Hill and Yeavering Bell.

CHATTON BRIDGE TO DODDINGTON BRIDGE

The R. Till now flows north-west below the Fell Sandstone escarpment on the side of Weetwood Hill and Dod Law, the latter being the highest point on Doddington Moor. There are flood embankments to protect the low-lying, flat farmland that broadens out at this point at the start of the Milfield Plain, the wide expanse of which is thought to have once been an ice-dammed lake (see p. 13). The town of Wooler is just over a mile to the south-west and the Wooler Water flows north-east through the town to join with and become a major tributary of, the Till. There are two obvious oxbow lakes along this stretch of the river. The strategic and landscape importance of the escarpment above is reflected in the number of prehistoric sites—a stone circle, hut circles, enclosures, settlements, forts, camps and many cup and ring marked rocks.

Here is also one of the two 'Cuddy's Caves' or 'St. Cuthbert's Caves', in Northumberland (the other is on St. Cuthbert's Way near Kyloe). This one, at Grid ref. NU00363101, is really a rock shelter formerly with cup and ring marks but also some unusual marks that may have been later in date and were recorded and drawn by George Tate in the 19th century before they were lost to view. Both caves or 'coves' are associated with St. Cuthbert who may have lived there as a hermit before moving to the Farne Islands; alternatively, his body may have been sheltered there when Bishop Eardulf removed it from Lindisfarne and wandered the countryside for seven years in order to protect the saint's remains during Viking raids.[18]

The river passes under Doddington Bridge at Grid Ref. NT99873077. The bridge carries the B6525 road north from Wooler, through Doddington and, eventually, to Scremerston, near Berwick.

Doddington Bridge from the west, with Doddington Moor in the distance.

There has been a bridge at Doddington since at least 1310 when a man accused of theft was caught there. Edward III is said to have stopped at Doddington in 1335 and may well have used the old bridge. If the Earl of Surrey and his army did not cross the Till at Weetwood, there would have been a bridge for them at Doddington. When Tony Dickens visited in 1975, the 19th century stone bridge had been out of use since 1948 when it was badly damaged by the huge floods that year. A temporary Bailey Bridge was built in 48 hours in 1948 with an estimated lifespan of eight years. In 1975, the Bailey Bridge was still there but there is now a modern, concrete bridge. There is still a section of fenced-off road, not visible in the photograph, which must have accessed the 'temporary' bridge.[19]

North of the river is the present village of Doddington. A fairly large, medieval village, first recorded in the 13th century when it was in the barony of Alnwick, stood to the south of the present village. It had over 160 adults in the 14th century but, today, the only remains survive as earthworks. In 1825, Eneas Mackenzie wrote that the parish contained 5 townships, 174 houses and 865 inhabitants. The soil was 'fertile and well cultivated, the annual value of property in this parish being, in 1815, estimated at £19,786'.

Of Doddington village, he said that it consisted:

principally of thatched cottages for labourers and colliers. The chapel belongs to the vicarage of Chatton, the duke of Northumberland being patron 1725. Here is a day-school and a Sunday-school, both of which are in a languishing state. Doddington was anciently one of the lordships of which the barony of Vescy, in Northumberland, consisted.[20]

The village, as opposed to the parish seems to have had a population of 339 in 1801, 419 in 1821 and 397 in 1851. 'Doddington' may be Anglo-Saxon in origin with 'tun' meaning 'farm'. Mawer gives a derivation of 'farm of Dodda or Dudda or of his sons'. Perhaps 'Dod' gave his name to 'Dod's Law' in which case it might have been a Celtic name.[21]

In the centre of the village at Grid Ref. NT99813250 are the ruins of what is probably an L-shaped bastle house rather than a bastle, on account of its larger size and more elaborate design. It was built in 1584 for Lord Grey of Chillingham and stood intact until 1896 when part of it collapsed in a gale; although now in a very ruined condition, conservation work has been carried out for its protection. It is a Grade II* listed, privately owned, building.[22] The church of St. Michael and St. George is a Grade I listed building and stands on the south-west side of the village at Grid. Ref. NT99573223. It is built on a 12th century site but the present structure is 13th century with 19th century alterations and additions. There is a watch-house in the churchyard built in 1826 to guard against body-snatchers supplying bodies for dissection by Scottish surgeons. In the porch, two ancient steles or grave covers have been built into the wall.

Almost opposite the village end of Drovers' Lane is the Grade II listed, Dod's Well, at Grid Ref. NT99933242. A spring issues from the base of a stone cross, erected by the Rev. Proctor in 1846. The well produces 70 gallons of water per minute and this quantity of constant, pure water which is thought to be fed to this and other wells (e.g. Cuddie's Well nearby) from acquifers from Dod Law would have been an incentive for the establishment of a settlement in Anglo-Saxon or earlier, times. There does not seem to be any religious association for Dod's Well except for the 19th century cross.

Doddington, unlike many villages that have lost facilities in recent times, is now renowned for the production of cheeses and ice-cream. It is also still home to Doddington Quarry just to the east of the village that has been producing sandstone since 1897. The stone produced here is of high quality, is fine-grained and has a pink to pale pink-purple colour. It is used in walling, masonry and facings for many buildings in Scotland, particularly in Edinburgh and in northern England, but can be found throughout the UK.

6

Doddington Bridge to Ford Bridge

Drovers' Lane becomes a rough track as it leaves the village in a south-westerly direction with the church, vicarage, watch house and graveyard on the right hand side. It is aptly named because it must have been an ancient track for cattle movement but it would also have provided a direct bridleway link between Doddington village and Ewart Park, crossing the R. Till by Cuthbertson's Bridge to the west of Doddington Bridge. The meandering river flows west to

R. Till looking north-west from Doddington Bridge.

north-west through unwooded pasture except for low trees and shrubs along its sand and gravel margins.

Cuthbertson's Bridge is just beyond where the small tributary runs into the river (just seen at top, left on the map below), a distance of less than a mile from Doddington Bridge. This tributary runs alongside Drovers' Lane and takes the outfalls from Dod's Well and surface water from elsewhere in the village.

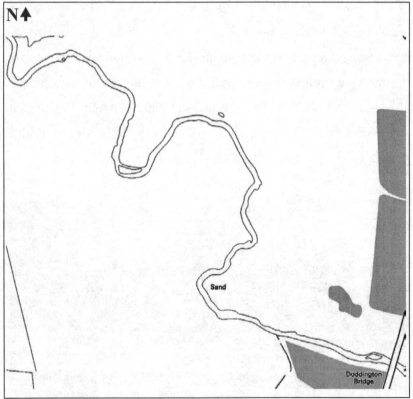

Doddington Bridge to Cuthbertson's Bridge. Distance-under 1mile. Contains Ordnance Survey data © Crown copyright and database right 2014.

After crossing Cuthbertson's Bridge, the bridleway also has to cross the R. Glen by way of the private Ewart Park Bridge.

Cuthbertson's Bridge from the east.

Cuthbertson's Bridge is a narrow, hump or hog-backed bridge at Grid Ref. NT98813162, listed Grade II and dated by English Heritage to the early 19th century although it may be older. It has a single arch of ashlar masonry with modern, blockwork parapets.[1] Tony Dickens states that Cuthbertson's or Cubberstone's (local name) Bridge is named after St. Cuthbert who is said to have spent some of his time in childhood as a shepherd in the neighbourhood.[2]

The bridge was badly damaged by floods in 2008 and is in a poor structural condition with many settlement cracks caused by erosion to the foundations. The construction of a new bridge, 25 m. south of the old bridge, was contracted out by Northumberland County Council and opened in March 2012. It comprises timber decking and handrails on tubular beams resting on precast abutments supported by tubular piles driven into the riverbanks. The old bridge, which was formerly used for farm traffic and the movement of sheep and cattle, has been closed off and its function taken over by the new bridge. The appearance of the new bridge, which has been engineered to withstand future flooding, nevertheless compares unfavourably with the fine, old, stone bridge.

The new bridge from the west.

About a mile to the north-west and downstream from Cuthbertson's Bridge, the R. Glen enters the Till from the south. This is the last major tributary to enter the Till before the latter enters the Tweed some considerable distance away. The R. Glen is a major tributary being fed by the Bowmont Water, which rises in the Scottish

Borders and by the College Burn which rises in the north Cheviot Hills before they both meet near Kirknewton.

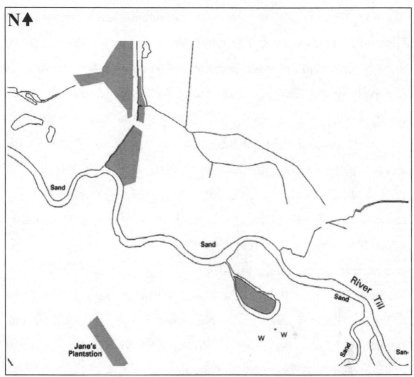

The R. Glen enters the R. Till in the bottom, right-hand corner. Jane's Plantation is below Ewart Park on the south side of the Till and the woodlands on the north side of the Till lead up to the farms and hamlet of Fenton. The distance from east to west across the map is about one mile. Contains Ordnance Survey data © Crown copyright and database right 2014.

Where the R. Glen meets the R. Till is reputed to be the site of King Arthur's first battle against the Anglo-Saxons, according to Nennius, a Welsh monk writing in the 9th century:

> Then it was, that the magnanimous Arthur, with all the kings and military force of Britain, fought against the Saxons. And though there were many more noble than himself, yet he was

133

twelve times chosen their commander, and was as often
conqueror. The first battle in which he was engaged, was at
the mouth of the river Gleni...[3]

There is some uncertainty as to whether Nennius was referring to the
Glem in Lincolnshire but J. A. Giles the editor and translator, favours
the R. Glen. In all the battles, the Britons triumphed, 'For no strength
can avail against the will of the Almighty'. Nennius was firmly on
Arthur's side.

As usual, I must not stray from my route to go further up the
valleys of the R. Glen, the Bowmont Water and the College Water
with all their archaeological and other sites—except to briefly
mention the Roman monk, Paulinus, who was sent to England by
Pope St. Gregory I ("the Great") to help St. Augustine. He
accompanied Aethelburh, the sister of King Eadbald of Kent when
she travelled to Northumbria to marry the pagan King Edwin (586-
633 AD). Paulinus was consecrated bishop before leaving Kent and,
eventually, he was successful in converting Edwin and a large number
of his people to Christianity. Bede wrote:

Once when Paulinus came to the king and queen in their royal
palace at Yeavering, he spent thirty-six days there occupied in
the task of catechizing and baptizing...When they [people
who had flocked to him from villages and districts] had
received instruction he washed them in the waters of
regeneration in the river Glen...[4]

Paulinus became Archbishop of York and died at Rochester in 644
AD. His name survives in the names of the house and estate at
Pallinsburn, near Cornhill-on-Tweed.

Well set back in the angle of the Till and the Glen lies the Ewart Park estate. The OE, *ea-weor*, means 'river-enclosure'.[5]

Eneas Mackenzie described Ewart as being:

> finely situate on the south side of the Till [north-west of the R. Glen]…It is supposed that a church formerly stood here, as one spot seems to have been used for a burial ground. *Ewart Park House* is a pleasant rural residence, and is the seat of Horace David Cholwell St. Paul, Bart.[6]

The Pauls originally came from Warwickshire and, in 1768, were granted, by Act of Parliament, the right to add 'Saint' to their name. Colonel Horace St. Paul (1729-1812) had left England for Austria in order to escape the death penalty following a duel. His military services were recognized by Empress Maria Theresa and he was made a Colonel of Cavalry and a Count of the Holy Roman Empire.

Colonel St. Paul's son, Sir Horace David Cholwell St. Paul (1775-1840) became 1st Baronet of Ewart Park and 2nd Count. He was married to Anna-Maria Ward (1778-1836), daughter of Viscount Dudley and Ward but was also friendly with two ladies of rank who were 'associated with him'. Altogether, he had 15 children. Sir Horace was in residence when Mackenzie wrote his description but in 1828, perhaps while Sir Horace was in the south of England as MP for Bridport, William Parson and William White stated that Ewart Park House was occupied by 'Mrs. Maria St. Paul, the lady of the manor, and relict of the late Henry Heneage St. Paul' the younger brother of Sir Horace.[7]

The 1st Baronet's son by Lady Anna-Maria was Sir Horace St. Paul, 2nd Baronet and 3rd Count (1812-1891). He married Jane Eliza

Grey (1842-1881), daughter of George Annett Grey of Milfield but the baronetcy died out with his death in 1891 because there was no son to succeed him. However, Sir Horace and Lady Jane had a daughter, Maria St. Paul (1868-1901) who inherited Ewart Park estate and married George Grey Butler (1852-1935); he suffered a riding accident, retired from the civil service and took over the running of the estate. He was descended on his mother's side from John Grey (1785-1868) of Milfield House and a cousin of the 2nd Earl Grey (1764-1845) who was Prime Minister.

John Grey's wife was Hannah Eliza Annett, daughter of Ralph Annett of Alnwick. George Grey Butler's father was George Butler (1819-1890) who became Headmaster of Liverpool College; his mother was the celebrated feminist writer, campaigner and welfare reformer, Josephine Butler (1828-1906), who supported the cause of fallen women and the repeal of the Contagious Diseases Acts.[8] There are memorials to the St. Paul family in the church of St. Mary and St. Michael, Doddington and also in the churchyard. I have only touched briefly on the histories of the families associated with Ewart Park until the early 20th century but sufficiently enough, I hope, to highlight the strong family connections by marriage and inheritance between the owners of the estates in north Northumberland. The names keep recurring in the stories of castles, bastles, pele towers, tower houses, country houses and estates.

Eneas Mackenzie mentions the discovery of two swords at Ewart Park:

In the beginning of February 1814, two ancient bronze sword blades were found in a grassy knowl in Ewart Park, only six inches below the surface. They were 21 inches long, and had been stuck down in a perpendicular position. The edges have angular gashes, which appear to have been made by similar weapons. They were in a fine state of preservation, the earth being a fine gravel. One of them was presented to the Antiquarian Society of Newcastle upon Tyne, by Mrs. St. Paul of Ewart, the lady of the manor.[9]

Mackenzie speculates on their origin. Matthew Culley, the agriculturalist, had suggested that they might have been dropped by stragglers from Flodden but Mackenzie knew that this was impossible and that the swords were much older than that even though he didn't know that they originated in the Bronze Age.

The significance of the find is recognized by the classification of 'Ewart Park Swords' as one of the nine types of Bronze Age sword found in England and Wales. The nine types cover a period from 1200 BC to 600 BC with the 'Ewart Park' type dating from 950 BC to 800 BC. Most Bronze Age swords in British museum collections come from the 'Ewart Park' period; they usually have a bulging shape in the blade at the midway point before narrowing at the shoulders and the terminal, which is fan-shaped.[10]

Ewart was renowned for the quality of its clay and there are surviving Grade II listed brick kilns dating from the late 18th or early 19th centuries that were used for brick-making.[11]

During WWII, Ewart Park was home to a military encampment; one of the battalions there for a time was the 7th King's Own Scottish Borderers, part of the 1st British Airborne Division which flew into Arnhem by glider.[12]

On the opposite side of the R. Till from Ewart are the farms and settlements of Fenton. On the modern OS map can be seen West Fenton, East Fenton, Fenton Hill, Fenton (House and Park) and Fenton Wood. There was a small village at Fenton in the 13th century when there were nine taxpayers and there was a tower in the 16th century when tenants were liable for Border service. The medieval village was west of the Old Grave Yard on the map below.[13]

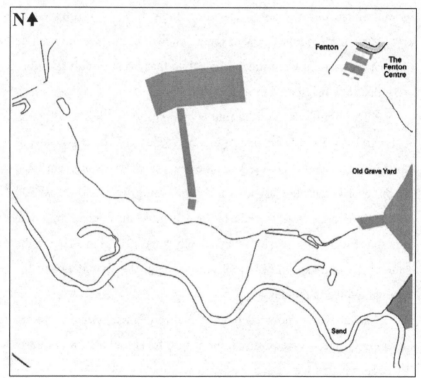

This is a continuation of the map on p. 133 showing West Fenton and the 'Old Grave Yard'. Distance from west to east is under 1mile. Contains Ordnance Survey data © Crown copyright and database right 2014.

Mawer gives the derivation of 'Fenton' as *fentun* meaning 'fen-farm and dwelling'.[14] Eneas Mackenzie wrote in 1825:

FENTON, a small village, the property of James Graham Clarke, Esq. is situate on the east side of the river Till, $3^3/_4$ miles north from Wooler, to which parish it belongs, though enclosed on all sides by the parish of Chatton. The Messrs. Culley farmed first at this place; and the improved state of the neighbourhood evinces the advantages that must always result from good example. It is now farmed by Mr. John Vardy and son, for whom a remarkably neat and convenient dwelling-house has been lately erected.[15]

Mackenzie was writing before the abolition of slavery. James Graham Clarke (1792-1857) was the son of John Graham Clarke, a prominent Newcastle businessman with interests in shipping, coal and in thirteen plantations in Jamaica. The Graham Clarke ships took Tyneside products such as coal, glass, pottery and linen to the New World and returned with sugar, rum and hardwoods. The sugar was refined in refineries in Newcastle, Stockton and Gateshead. After the Abolition of Slavery Act 1833, plantation owners were able to claim compensation from a government fund of £20 M for the loss of slaves until the scheme was abolished in 1838. James and his father's friend, James Lamb, as trustees and executors of John Graham Clarke, claimed for 271 slaves on the Bamboo Sugar Estates in Jamaica, for which they were awarded £4,968. 12s. 3d in March 1837.[16]

Alnwick Abbey owned Fenton Parish in the 12th century and a chapel was in existence in the 14th century with ruins still visible until the early 19th century. There are no longer any visible remains. Until 1960, West Fenton was known as Fenton Demesne and East Fenton (an 1830 Grade II listed building) was just known as Fenton.

'Demesne' is the feudal term for that portion of the manor reserved by the lord for his own use and not that of his serfs or tenants. In the past, there was a millpond and two watermills at or near East Fenton.[17]

There are the sites of two Iron Age forts to the north-east of East and West Fenton. The first is at Fenton Hill Camp, next to Fenton Hill Farm; this was built in three stages, the first, pallisaded enclosure between the late Bronze Age and early Iron Age, replaced by a single rampart with timber revetment and ditch and finally, the addition of inner and outer ramparts. Two timber round houses were inside. The other fort, North Fenton Hill 2 Enclosure, had three ditches and had hut circles inside.[18]

On the opposite side of the R. Till from Fenton, I have already mentioned the estate of Ewart Park. To the north of Ewart are two very large properties, Galewood and Thirlings. Both of the houses are Grade II listed buildings and, in the 19th century, formed part of the Ewart Park estate owned by the St. Paul family. Galewood became the home of George Grey Butler after he had had retired from the Civil Service following his accident. His father, George, died in 1890 and, in 1894, his mother, Josephine Butler, went to live at Galewood with her son who had tried to carry on his work as an examiner to the Civil Service Commissioners but had had to retire in 1895. In a letter dated 1st June 1894 to her friends, the Priestmans, Josephine writes, 'George's work people and gardener are already preparing Galewood for the family to come to about the middle of July 1894, to leave Wart to be cleaned etc.' She also hoped to get to Cornhill-on-Tweed where the Butlers often stayed when her husband was alive. By 24th July, Josephine writes from Galewood that George is still very weak, 'I am sorry about my dear George...it was a cruel accident'.[19]

There was a well-regarded pack of hounds at Galewood. *The New Sporting Magazine* for May 1834 says:

The Galewood (Major St. Paul's) are reported to be a very flourishing and improving pack and it is said that Lord Ossulston [became 6th Earl of Tankerville in 1859] purports hunting with them during the early part of the season.[20]

In the mid 19th century, the remains of possibly two Anglo-Saxon or early medieval bodies were found at Galewood with two bronze rings, a pottery vessel and two iron spearheads.[21]

The late 18th or early 19th century house, Thirlings, was built by Count St. Paul and extended and given Italianate detailing between 1860-1870.[22] The derivation of 'Thirlings' is uncertain. It may come from an Old English verb, *thyrelian*, to drill or pierce or bore, which may refer to pits or post holes, *thyrel* holes from Anglo-Saxon times; there is also a possible engineering or mining connotation whereby 'thirlings' refer to tunnels or shafts. Alternatively, the word may refer to a feudal practice whereby someone is bound in a form of servitude to give the results of his work to another, perhaps by the milling of corn (in a thirl-mill), although this may have applied more in Scotland. This meaning, which may or may not be relevant here, is described in detail in Erskine's *Law of Scotland*.[23]

Thirlings is more widely known for its importance as an archaeological site with evidence of 6th century occupation having been discovered from cropmarks by St. Joseph and McCord and excavated between 1973 and 1981 by Miket and O'Brien who also discovered evidence of Neolithic occupation. Evidence of 12 timber buildings was found dating from the early medieval period; two of these had their own fenced compounds suggesting some better status. There was no boundary fence. Of the 12 buildings, three were smaller than the other nine which, although not as large as the large halls at Yeavering, were still at the larger end of the scale when compared with other sites of this period elsewhere in England. The inhabitants were probably farmers and carbon dating of construction timber remains showed that the site was founded in the mid to late 6th century and continued to be used until the 7th century by which time the Anglian kingdom of Bernicia was well-established. It is not known whether the inhabitants were Anglian or were native British but there was no evidence of any attack on the settlement and, by the 7th century there is likely to have been a merging of ethnic groups.[24]

In chapter 1 (p. 13) and in the last chapter (p. 125), I referred to the post-glacial lake that once occupied part of the Milfield plain. The latter stretches from Wooler in the south to Etal in the north and forms a basin between the Cheviot Hills on the south and west sides and the sandstone escarpment on the east and north sides. The silt and sediment trapped behind the dammed-up lake together with more recent sediments has created a fertile area, attractive to farmers since prehistoric times. The area is open, giving plenty of sunlight for the growing of crops or for pasture whilst rainfall that might otherwise be excessive, is heavier in the surrounding hills. This is a land rich in archaeology with hill forts on the hills overlooking the plain and evidence of settlements, henges and other signs of extensive human occupation to be found on the plain.

DODDINGTON BRIDGE TO FORD BRIDGE

The area to the north-west of Galewood and Thirlings changed dramatically during the 20th century. In 1917, a field at Woodbridge Farm was chosen by 77 Squadron of Edinburgh as a landing and refuelling site for patrols in southern Scotland but this was discontinued in 1919. In 1940, a large area was developed as a Fighter Command training facility with a triangular arrangement of runways and dispersed buildings to minimize casualties in the event of enemy attack. In 1942, RAF Milfield became a low attack instructors' school using Hurricane and Hawker Typhoon aircraft and, in 1944, when the Fighter Leaders' School was formed, RAF Milfield trained many of the pilots that flew ground attack Hawker Typhoon aircraft after the D-Day landings in Normandy. In the same year, the Fighter Leaders' School was joined by a squadron of USAAF aircraft including the P-47 Thunderbolt, the P-38 Lightning and the P-51 Mustang.[25] In 1968, part of the disused airfield that was not being used for quarrying, together with additional land from Galewood, enabled the formation of the Borders Gliding Club which now states that it has some of the finest facilities in the UK.

In the 1970s and beyond, gravel and course sand deposits were quarried by Tarmac from under the 250-acre airfield site at Woodbridge. The final phase of the site, known as Woodbridge Quarry, has been completed with two-thirds given over to a mosaic of wildlife habitats and one-third to agriculture. The restoration was carried out by Tarmac in partnership with Northumberland County Council, Natural England and Northumberland Wildlife Trust. There are hedges, trees, swamps and pebbly areas for nesting. There is grassland seeded with a wildflower mix and wetlands with shallow

143

margins that expand and contract during wet and dry periods to increase feeding opportunities for wading birds and to attract insects and amphibians. Between 2005 and 2011, the number of bird species recorded had increased from 24 to 42 and included wildfowl, over-wintering ducks, teal, wigeon, shelduck, snipe, lapwing, oystercatcher and ringed plover in the varied habitats at Woodbridge. Brown hare, otter and common toads are also in residence. A 10-year aftercare management scheme is in operation.[26]

In 2005, Archaeological Research Services Ltd., on behalf of Tarmac Northern Ltd. (Phase 1) and English Heritage (Phase 2) were able to excavate 4.5 hectares of land on the eastern side of Cheviot Quarry adjacent to Woodbridge Farm. Evidence was found for Neolithic, Late Bronze Age and 'Dark Age' settlements. The Neolithic pottery, lithics and cereal grains taken with Neolithic finds from Thirlings and the nearby Lanton Quarry (see next page) show significant occupation on the Milfield plain. It is suggested that the sites are precursors to the ceremonial 'henge' complex located nearby which dates to the Beaker period. Material attached to the ceramics provide some of the earliest evidence of dairy farming in the area as well as information on diet.

Two large roundhouses with hearths and domestic refuse pits provided evidence of late Bronze Age lowland settlement for which there was also evidence suggesting arable and pastoral activity in a small, unenclosed farming settlement. Carbon dating of three rectangular buildings came up with the 5th or early 6th century AD but a lack of other material has prevented a definitive view as to their use. They may have been agricultural homesteads occupied by native

Britons or by early Anglo-Saxon settlers. [27] At the nearby Maelmin Heritage Trail, a short walk takes visitors past a reproduction of a wooden henge from 2000 BC, a Mesolithic hut and a 'Dark Age' hut similar to the one found at Tarmac's Cheviot Quarry.[28] 'Maelmin' (now Milfield) is mentioned by Bede as the successor palace to ad Gefrin which was abandoned in the 7th century in the time of the Saxon kings of Bernicia who followed King Edwin (616-632).[29] Fox suggests that it might derive from *moel*, 'bare' and *mynedd*, 'hill' but also quotes another interpretation, *mael*, 'prince' and *min*, 'edge'. Whichever it may be, the name will be Brythonic in origin.[30]

Another nearby archaeological excavation is at Lanton Quarry fronting the A697 road to the south-west of Ewart Park and adjacent to a wooded part of the estate with radiating paths known as 'The Wilderness'. This excavation has been carried out by Archaeological Research Services Ltd. (excavation director Dr. Clive Waddington) on behalf of Tarmac Northern Ltd. It comprises two phases of 9.5 hectares and 1.5 hectares. Phase 1 uncovered evidence of Neolithic settlement including four trapezoidal structures, three triangular structures and associated hearths and pits. There was one Bronze Age roundhouse probably in association with two rectangular structures and one possible Iron Age roundhouse with large associated pits. At the southern half of the site, there was a concentration of early medieval settlement including two rectangular and two square post-built buildings, six sunken feature buildings and associated pits and postholes.

Phase 2 results included seven, post-built structures including one circular and two, rectangular structures, twenty-two pits, some of them with burning and some of which had pottery, nineteen isolated postholes, a linear feature thought to be a post-medieval field boundary and two possible Bronze Age stone-built cists, one of them containing human remains. The cist containing human remains was the least disturbed and was built of 73 different sized, but mainly flat, Cheviot stones, set in a corbelled arrangement and with cap stones. The skull was resting on a flat stone but there were no grave goods.[31]

The Maelmin Trail is at the north-west end of the former airfield and the R. Till flows past on the north-east side to pass under Redscar Bridge at Grid ref. NT94623370.

Redscar Bridge, south-east face.

The iron girder bridge is not the original construction but neither is it a recent one, as a postcard from 1903 shows it to have been in place at that time. Newcastle University's SINE Project

(Structural Images of the North East) records a stone bridge having been built in 1813 following a Renewal Act of 1812 which included provision for a link from the Milfield to Wooler Road, crossing the Till by a new bridge at Redscar to be built by the turnpike trustees and passing through Kimmerston and by Ford Colliery to join the Ford to Barmoor road.[32] The bridge fell down in 1814 and it was recorded that 'it fell down with a tremendous crash. The architect who was below removing some props, was unfortunately killed, being buried in the ruins'.[33] The bridge was replaced by a wooden structure.

Red Scar Bridge, Millfield

Postcard showing Redscar Bridge, dated August 9th 1903. Author's collection.

Redscar Bridge (perhaps the wooden one) was there in 1843 because Tony Dickens tells of an auction to find the highest bidder for the tolls, held at the house of Mr. Chrystal, Delaval's Arms Inn, Ford on 24th October 1843. The tolls raised for the previous year were £76 and Dickens thought this to be low, suggesting low usage.[34] The SINE records have a photograph taken in 1972 showing the approach to a ford on the south-east side of the bridge.

The approach road to the Redscar Bridge from the north-east, Kimmerston side, also crosses a long, flat bridge that straddles the flood plain. This is the Redscar Flood Relief Bridge built in 1953 (see map on p. 149) at the request of the former Northumberland River Board because of the extensive flooding at this point. Its construction is of reinforced concrete and it has 14 spans and 13 piers.[35] The bridge is purely functional and it has no aesthetic appeal.

The need for such a long bridge crossing a flood plain at this point emphasizes the fact that this section of the R. Till has a low gradient as it crosses the Milfield plain. In Chapter 3 (see pp. 67-8), I touched on the detailed and ambitious strategy in the *River Till Restoration Strategy* drawn up by Natural England, the Environment Agency and the Tweed Forum in March 2013. This identifies the current condition of the rivers in the Till Catchment SSSI, identifies the problems, sets out the potential solutions with costs and gives a 25-30 year delivery timescale.

Of the six river types shown in the *Strategy's* Figure 5, the Milfield plain stretch is classified as 'Low gradient active meandering'; in Table 8, the summary of potential restoration options identified by reach (i.e stretch of river), the Milfield plain reaches are given a high priority for action. Remedial work that is needed now on all reaches of the river system is often necessary because of human activity in the past. Historic, localised bank protection will often affect natural flow patterns and exacerbate erosion elsewhere. Similar problems can be caused by channel realignment or by introducing

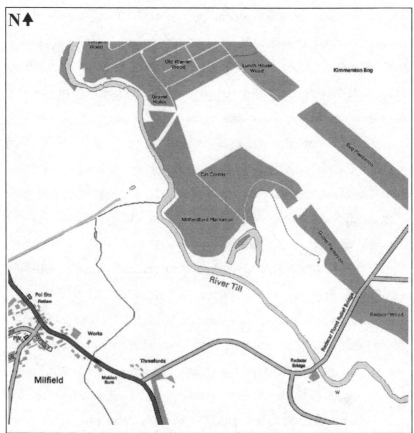

Milfield, Redscar Bridge and Redscar Flood Relief Bridge. Distance from west to east across the map, about 1 mile. Contains Ordnance Survey data © Crown copyright and database right 2014.

weirs or by over-deepening channels. Damage can be caused by allowing stock to have access to riverbanks, or run-off from agricultural land may cause excessive deposits of sediments. Human intervention can also cause obstruction to fish movement, particularly the upstream migration of salmon, sea trout, eel and lamprey.

Taking only one reach of the R. Till across the Milfield plain as an example, the reach from Redscar Bridge to Ford Bridge has

149

restoration priorities from medium to high in the *Strategy*. Restoration options include the realignment or setting back of floodbanks to create erodible corridors; lowering or breaching to reconnect channel to flood plain; improved floodwater evacuation; removal of hardbank protection and possible installation of soft engineering; removal or modification of weirs and much more.

This simplification does not do justice to the very detailed analysis and solutions set out in the *Strategy* but it is encouraging to note the work that has been put into it by the agencies and their determination to protect and improve the R. Till system. As always, the main constraint is finance[36]

Eneas Mackenzie described Milfield as 'a small, well-built village, the property of Earl Grey...In the 10th of Elizabeth, 1568, Oswald Muschampe held the village of Milfield'. He then mentions it as the place of residence of the Saxon kings after Edwin and goes on:

> On the south side of the village is a large and beautiful plain, famous for the defeat of a large body of Scots before the battle of Flodden [1513], by Sir William Bulmer, of Brancepeth Castle, who commanded the forces of the bishopric of Durham. The Scots had concealed themselves among the broom, which then covered the plain. Five or six hundred of them were killed, and four hundred taken prisoners. They afterwards called the road through the plain the ill road. There is a Sunday school at Milfield, which is well attended.[37]

In relation to the Muschampe family, *The Gentleman's Magazine* in 1822 records that:

Coupland [situated south-west of Milfield on the R. Glen], in the time of Henry III, was a manor in the barony of Muschamp [sic], of whom William of Akild held Akyld, Coupland, and Yever, by one knight's fee of the old feoffment.[38]

The present Coupland Castle (a Grade I listed building) is a tower house that was built in the 16th century by the Wallis family. In the 18th century, it was owned by Nathaniel Ogle and was restored in the 19th century by Thomas Bates. It is a private house but it is open to the public for weddings and guided tours, by arrangement.

A previous battle in the vicinity of Milfield was the battle of Homildon Hill in 1402 when the Scottish Earl of Douglas, on his way back from a successful plundering raid as far south as Newcastle, was caught up by the Earl of Northumberland and his son, Hotspur. This was a battle won by the English archers who devastated the Scottish forces who remained in position without fighting. In 1856, William Whellan & Co.'s *History etc.* refers to Fordun's account (Walter Bower's continuation of John of Fordun's *Scotichronicum*, c.1440) and how, finally:

> Swinton, a spirited knight, induced this movement [a Scottish charge down the hill] by exclaiming—"Oh! My brave fellow soldiers, what fascinates you today, that you stand like deer and fawns in a park to be shot, instead of showing your ancient valour, and meeting your foes hand to hand?"[39]

It was too late as Douglas was wounded and there was a rout of his army; according to Whellans, five hundred Scots even drowned in the Tweed, presumably whilst fleeing back home.

Milfield today, is a small, thriving, rural community that also enjoys passing trade from the A697 road and benefits from visitors to The Maelmin Trail. There is a post office/general store, a food processing company, a country café and a public house.

The R. Till flows north-west from Redscar Bridge, passing Milfield and adopting a meandering course alongside wooded plantations on the right hand bank before gradually turning to the north and then north-east before reaching Ford Bridge. The river also flows past the eastern flank of Flodden Hill, the encampment (with the ridge to the west) of the Scottish army before the Battle of Flodden, 1513. This is not the place to describe the battle, which has received much literary (both fiction and non-fiction) and commemorative attention in recent times, much of it coinciding with the 500th anniversary of the battle in 2013. Without adding to the literature, there is no doubt that the R. Till has an important topographical connection with Flodden because it skirts the eastern flank of the battlefield site and had to be crossed by the English army prior to the engagement. The river also featured in the movements of the English army earlier on, as it moved north, crossing the Till at Weetwood or Doddington on the way north to the final camp before the battle, at Barmoor.

The stretch of river below Redscar Bridge is one of four main fishing beats on the Ford & Etal Estates and is an 'easy' beat to fish with good access and level walks on the river bank. It has 15 named pools over $1\frac{1}{2}$ miles and these are defined by the estate as being long and deep (4 to 8 feet) but not fast running, consisting of glides (the most predictable and smooth running kind of 'river swim'). The R.

DODDINGTON BRIDGE TO FORD BRIDGE

Till is well known for its run of sea trout during the season from 1st February to 30th November but grilse and salmon (same season) are also taken, as are grayling in winter. The spring salmon season is from 1st February to 30th June. There is also a natural stock of non-migratory brown trout to be caught from March to September.

R. Till north-west of Redscar Bridge, looking towards Milfieldford Plantation.

Usually, any angler in England aged 12 years and over, fishing for salmon, trout, freshwater fish or eels requires an Environment Agency rod licence but the R. Till, because it is a tributary of the R. Tweed, is classed as a Scottish river in terms of control and administration and comes under the jurisdiction of the River Tweed Commission through the Scotland Act 1998 (River Tweed) Order 2006, with conduct subject to the *Tweed Angling Code*.

153

BREAMISH AND TILL: FROM SOURCE TO TWEED

The Tweed Commission retains responsibility for policing and administration of fishings within the Tweed catchment and delegates the scientific aspects of stock management to the Tweed Foundation through *The Tweed Fisheries Management Plan*. The Tweed Foundation was set up in 1983 and is a charitable trust with the trustees tasked to promote the development of salmon and trout stocks throughout the Tweed system through biological research, stock monitoring and habitat enhancement. This is an example of cross-border (Scotland/England) integration that benefits the river system as a whole.

Another example of cross-border co-operation is seen in the work of the Tweed Forum, the membership of which comprises organizations on both sides of the R. Tweed and on both sides of the border. The Forum was established in 1991 'to promote the wise and sustainable use of the Tweed and its tributaries through holistic and integrated management and planning'. The Forum is able to lead on projects such as the Tweed Invasives Project set up in 2002, tackling such problems as the invasion of giant hogweed, *Heracleum mantegazzianum*, Japanese knotweed, *Fallopia japonica* and Himalayan balsam, *Impatiens glandulifera*. But the Tweed Invasives Project is only one of fifty constituent projects of the overall Tweed Rivers Heritage Project which is implemented by the partnership between the Tweed Forum's thirty or so members.

The relationships between the various bodies may seem complicated, but new legislation requires even more cross-border planning and co-operation. For example, the European Union's Water Framework Directive sets a framework for enhancing the water

154

environment from 2009 until 2015 with some commitments possibly extending to 2021 or 2027. In southern Scotland and northern England this is translated into the *Solway Tweed River Basin Management Plan* prepared by the Scottish Environment Protection Agency (SEPA) for Scotland and the Environment Agency for England. For the Tweed catchment part of the Plan, the Tweed Forum's Executive Committee and other organizations from Scotland and England, meet as the Tweed Area Advisory Group to progress the *Tweed Area Management Plan.*

As regards fishing the Till, Thomas Tod Stoddart, writing in 1847, said of the Till:

> It is a deep, sluggish water, singularly fantastic in its windings. The fish it contains are pike, perch, trout, and eels; but the migratory sort, especially whitlings [small sea-trout in their first year after smolt migration], enter it freely, and much earlier than they do any other branch from the main stream [The R. Tweed]. Not many salmon, however, are caught by the rod above Etal, their progress being much obstructed by a waterfall in that locality. The sea-trout, on the occurrence of a flood, force their way up into the Glen...The Glen is in high repute as an angling stream, and contains abundance of small, lively trout...Connected with this district is the Glendale fishing-club [now the Glendale Grayling Club, founded in 1838], a numerous body of Northumbrians, comprising several able and intelligent anglers.[40]

Since 1847, engineering works have made it easier for the passage of fish. Also, Stoddart does not mention grayling which is not an indigenous species and was only introduced to the Tweed catchment in the late 1800s. Its existence was kept a secret for a long time but now, 'The Lady of the Stream' is valued as a game fish after the salmon/trout season has ended.

There are no longer any perch in the Till, these being confined to lochs and pools, and pike would only be an occasional catch but trout and salmon thrive in addition to grayling. Eels and lamprey are to be found although the former is in decline. The trout, *Salmo trutta*, has two alternative life cycles. The first is the freshwater form known as brown trout and the second is the sea trout which is not a separate species but a migratory form of the brown trout with a life cycle similar to the Atlantic salmon, *Salmo salar*, in that it migrates to sea in order to feed and grow and then returns to fresh water to spawn. The brown trout does have a migratory pattern but spends all of its life in fresh water.

There are three species of lamprey, the brook lamprey, *Lampetra planeri*, the river lamprey, *Lampetra fluviatilis* and the sea lamprey, *Petromyzon marinus*, the sea lamprey being the largest of the species, reaching up to one metre in length. They resemble eels in having a long, cylindrical body; they have a skeleton of cartilage, no fish scales, a single nostril on top of the head, seven sac-like gills opening on each side of the head and primitive mouthparts surrounded by a flexible lip that acts as a sucker—hence the scientific name for the sea lamprey, *Petromyzon*, meaning stone sucker.

The brook lamprey is an entirely freshwater species growing to a length of 15-19 cm., whereas the river lamprey migrates from its coastal feeding grounds into fresh water for spawning and can grow to

30-50 cm. Most species of lamprey are parasitic and feed on other fish.

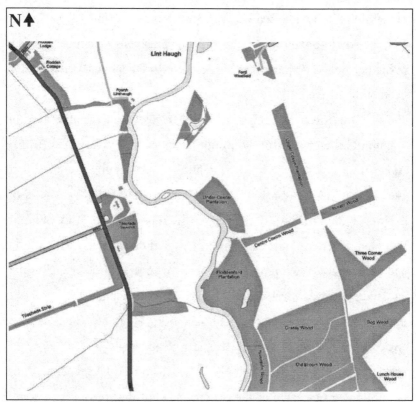

Continuation northwards of map on p. 149. Distance from west to east across the map, about 1 mile. Contains Ordnance Survey data © Crown copyright and database right 2014.

On the first edition of the OS map, there is a ford shown crossing the Till at Floddenford Plantation opposite a small tributary that runs into the Till from the west. It has been suggested that this might date from the Roman era.[41] A short distance to the south-west, on the open land to the west of the river, is the site of a Bronze Age henge consisting of a circular ditch within which is a circle of 30 small pits that once held upright wooden posts. The entrance was aligned towards the Cheviot Hills and, as there are eight such henge sites in the Till valley, it is possible that they formed some kind of processional way focused on, say, the prominent hill of Yeavering Bell. In Anglo-Saxon times, the site was reused as a cemetery.[42] This particular henge is known as Milfield North Henge and a replica has been built at Maelmin.

Other nearby henges are the Milfield South Henge and the Whitton Hill Henge. Milfield South Henge was also from the Bronze Age with a circular ditch and a central pit containing a cup-marked stone. Again, Anglo-Saxon remains were found here. This site is on the west side of the A697 road, opposite the Maelmin Trail. Whitton Hill Henge is north-east of Milfield Hill and dates from the Neolithic and Bronze Ages. Cropmarks have shown several circular enclosures and there were several central burial pits surrounded by a circular ditch. There were at least 26 burials from Neolithic times and an enclosure that was probably a Bronze Age barrow.[43]

The map on p. 157 shows Tilesheds Sawmill, opened in 1964 but no longer operating as the original sawmill business even if some use is being made of the land. This is the site of the former Flodden Brick and Tile Works which, on the first edition of the OS map (after 1856), shows the tile works with Tilework Cottages to the south, behind which was a pit. The business was established by the owner of Ford Estate, Sir John Hussey Delaval in 1768 and provided bricks and pantiles for the estate. By 1771, it is said that 100,000 bricks were being produced together with the same number of pantiles. Later, the works made other products as well and it is said that a number of ornamental clay cannons were made here for the postern lodge of Ford Castle.[44] An invoice for 1894 recently auctioned online shows that the firm then running the works was James Moffat & Sons. The works seem to have closed by about 1900 and, although 'Flodden Tile Works' is still labelled as such on the OS map after 1919, the buildings had been demolished and replaced by curling ponds that survived until at least the 1950s and perhaps until the establishment of the sawmill.

On the corner of the A697 road and the B6354 road, is Flodden Lodge, a Grade II listed, two storey, stone and slate building built for the Marchioness of Waterford, probably by David Bryce. It is just visible in the top left-hand corner of the map on p. 157. There is a moulded panel above the porch door with the date 1865 and the Waterford monogram.[45] The R. Till swings round past the rear of Flodden Lodge and past Flodden Westfield on the other bank where a Bronze Age dagger was found.[46] In a field behind Flodden Lodge and near Second Linthaugh, is the site of a henge and there is the site of another on the north side of the B6354 road, beyond First Linthaugh.[47] The R. Till runs next to the B6354 road for a short distance and, just before the 'T' junction with the B6353 road, it turns sharply north-west to pass under Ford Bridge. Ford Bridge, Grid Ref. NT93913746, is situated in line with the western entrance to Ford Castle and the single-storey West Lodge, the octagonal gate pillars and the impressive screen walls, are listed Grade II. The lodge, walls and gate pillars were built in 1866 for the Marchioness of Waterford whose monogram is on the gable and the prancing horses on the gate pillars were added by Lord Joicey after 1907.[48]

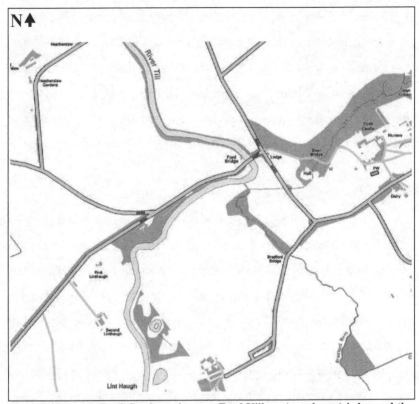

Ford Bridge with Ford Castle to the east. Ford Village (not shown) is beyond the castle. Distance from west to east across the map is a little over 1 mile. Contains Ordnance Survey data © Crown copyright and database right 2014.

In 1769, there is an early reference to Ford Bridge by John Wallis in his *Antiquities of Northumberland* 'We cross the *Till* at *Ford* by a stone-bridge of one large and strong arch...'[49] This is not the same bridge as the present one which Tony Dickens says was probably reconstructed c. 1865, following a petition in 1864 to the Justices of Northumberland in Quarter Sessions asking that the bridge should be widened.[50] However, another source says that the bridge that was already there in 1769, seems to have collapsed in 1807 and

160

was rebuilt in 1807-9 with two arches. It is also suggested that this bridge may have incorporated one of the arches from an earlier bridge perhaps dating to the 16th century.[51] Whatever the real story, any earlier construction would seem to have been hidden by the 1865 reconstruction. The bridge now has two arches and a flood arch built in masonry and strengthened by tie-bars because of the heavy traffic; the tie-bars have been in place for some time.

Ford Bridge from the south. The tie-bars can be seen on the left side.

Ford Bridge and the road junction were obviously selected as being suitable for defence in case of invasion during WWII because there are the remains of a dug-out and two pillboxes sited around the junction and behind the lodge, as well as the remains of 'dragon's teeth' concrete road blocks, one of which has fallen in the river.[52]

East of the bridge is Ford Castle and Ford Village. In the 13th century, Ford was in the manor of Odonel de Ford who married the youngest daughter of Robert de Muschampe, Baron of Wooler. It passed to Sir William Heron, whose mother was the daughter and heir of Odonel de Ford. A descendant, another Sir William Heron, 'embattled' the mansion-house under a licence granted by Edward III and was also granted the right to hold it *per nomen castri* for the defence of the area against the Scots.

The castle remained in the Heron family but was destroyed by the Scots in 1385 before William Heron returned to rebuild it. In 1388, the castle was taken by Henry Lilburn who had imprisoned William Heron, but Heron was able to recapture it after receiving his freedom. In 1430, another William Heron was killed by John Manners in an attack on Etal Castle and Ford Castle was destroyed again. Ford was repaired by Sir Roger Heron but, in 1513, it was captured and burnt down by James IV of Scotland prior to his defeat at the Battle of Flodden. Elizabeth Heron, daughter of the William Heron killed by John Manners, married Thomas Carr who took possession of the castle until his claim was disputed by the Herons of Chipchase, resulting in legal dispute and physical conflict. The Herons won the dispute and Thomas Carr was murdered at Ford Castle.

The castle passed by marriage to the Carrs and Robert Hugill in his *Borderland Castles and Peles* says that this was in romantic circumstances. It seems that the young Thomas Carr put up a spirited and successful defence of one of the towers against a Scottish Force under the Sieur d'Éssé, a brilliant French commander who had destroyed most of the castle with four guns. The heiress was much taken with Thomas Carr and they were married, but not before a spat between the Herons (who sent an armed group to retain Ford) and the Carrs, who ambushed the Herons. During the affray, the mayor of Berwick, who was a Heron supporter, was killed 'with xv blodye wounds upon him'. In 1662, the estate passed to Sir Francis Blake (1638-1718) on his marriage to Elizabeth Carr.[53]

For much of the time the castle had been in a ruinous state but Sir Francis Blake built a mansion within the castle. Ford Castle was inherited by Sir Francis's grandson, Captain Francis Blake Delaval (1692-1752), who added Delaval to his name when he inherited the Delaval Estates at Seaton and elsewhere. The Delaval Estates passed, first of all to his eldest son, Sir Francis Blake Delaval (1727-1771) and then to his second son, Sir John Hussey Delaval (1728-1808), 1st Baron Delaval who carried out major alterations starting in 1761. Eneas Mackenzie says of Sir John Hussey Delaval that:

> [his] memory is highly honoured in Northumberland. He employed his ample wealth in cultivating and improving his estates, and in dispensing felicity to innumerable families. The country around Ford, which was one continued sheep-walk, he divided and inclosed with excellent hedges, and clothed the bare hills with fine plantations. He also attempted to increase the riches and population of the country by the establishment of a plating-forge, which he erected in 1769, about a mile further down the river, where a large quantity of shovels, spades, etc. were made, as well as for home consumption as for exportation. Had the scheme succeeded according to the benevolent views of its proprietor, it would

have been productive of many beneficial consequences to this district.

The last sentence was premature as Ford Forge (see pp. 171-5) continued operating until 1897, with spades still being assembled there until the 1920s.

Eneas Mackenzie also speaks with affection of Lady Delaval, the second wife of Sir John Hussey Delaval. She had a life interest in the estate and her death in 1822 was recent enough for Mackenzie, in 1825, to say, 'The amiable and beneficent character of this excellent lady will be long remembered and revered in Northumberland'.[54]

Ford Castle today, viewed from the B6353 road.

As his son had predeceased him, the title became extinct and Sir John Hussey Delaval, apart from his wife's life interest, left the

164

estate to his daughter, Sarah Hussey, Countess of Tyrconnel, whose only daughter, Lady Susanna Carpenter (d. 1827), married Henry de La Poer Beresford, 2nd Marquess of Waterford (1772-1826), who assumed the estate.

The estate passed to the 2nd Marquess's son, Henry de La Poer Beresford, 3rd Marquess of Waterford (1811-1859) who married Louisa Anne Stuart (1818-1891). There were no children of the marriage and Lady Louisa Beresford, Marchioness of Waterford, a highly accomplished Pre-Raphaelite artist and philanthropist, concentrated her efforts on the welfare of her tenants and the improvement of the Ford Estate, as described later on. She was responsible for the restoration of the castle by David Bryce from 1862 onwards. In 1907, Ford Estate was purchased by the 1st Baron Joicey of Chester-le-Street, a very successful businessman and owner of coal-mines in Durham. In 1908, Lord Joicey purchased the adjoining Etal Estate. Today, The Rt. Hon. Lord Joicey, (5th Baron Joicey) is the principal Trustee of Ford & Etal Estates.

Ford Castle is a Grade I listed building which, from 1956 until 2012, was operated by Northumberland County Council as an outdoor activity centre and, since then, as a centre for residential school trips in a joint venture between the Council and a private company.[54]

St. Michael and All Angels church stands in the grounds of Ford Castle and has always been linked to it. The present patron is Lord Joicey. The church, which is a Grade II* listed building, was built in the 13th century, as was the original castle, and it was restored and enlarged during the 19th century by the Newcastle architect, John

165

Dobson.[55] The grave of Louisa, Lady Waterford, is in the churchyard; the gravestone was made by the renowned 19th century artist, G. F. Watts in 1891. Nearby are the remains of 'Parson's Tower', a 16th century or earlier dwelling which was demolished by the 17th century and later replaced by a rectory that was partly demolished in the 19th century. The Parson's Tower is listed as Grade II.[56]

Ford Village, to the east of the castle, is medieval, but was remodelled by Louisa, Lady Waterford, before her death in 1891. Her husband, the 4th Marquess, died from a riding accident in 1859 and the fountains and flower beds in the centre of the village were erected by Lady Waterford in his memory. The village and the estate contain attractive houses built for the estate workers and a school was provided in 1860 by Lady Waterford which she decorated internally with her own biblical paintings using members of the community as models. The school closed in 1957 and was renamed The Lady Waterford Hall, now run by a charitable trust set up to display her paintings and other artwork; the hall is open to the public.

I am conscious that I have still not moved down-river from Ford Bridge but this is because there is so much to see and discover in the vicinity of the bridge. For example, in addition to Ford castle and Ford Village, there is the interesting Ford Moss, under two miles to the east of the village. This is a lowland raised peat bog that lies between farmland to the north and the fell sandstone ridge to the south. It is within a hollow and the Moss has grown over a small lake formed after the last ice age. The site is managed by the Northumberland Wildlife Trust in partnership with Ford & Etal Estates. The Moss is composed of a thick layer of peat that has built up over many years and much of it has dried out to allow the growth of heather. On the wetter parts, there is sphagnum moss, *Sphagnum*, round-leaved sundew, *Drosera rotundifolia*, cranberry, *Vaccinium oxycoccus*, cross-leaved heath, *Erica tetralix*, bog-myrtle, *Myrica gale* and hare's tail cotton grass, *Eriophorum vaginatum*. The large heath butterfly, *Coenonympha tullia*, the small copper butterfly, *Lycaena phlaes* and the orange tip butterfly, *Anthocharis cardamines*, are there and there are common lizards, *Zootoca vivipara* and adders, *Vipera berus*. Birds include red grouse, *Lagopus lagopus scotica*, meadow pipit, *Anthus pratensis*, woodcock, *Scolopax*, snipe, *Gallinago gallinago*, buzzard, *Buteo buteo* and kestrel, *Falco tinnunculus*.[57]

This is also the site of the former Ford Moss Colliery that would have existed in a completely different industrial landscape compared with today's tranquil scene. Coal was worked here from at least the mid 17th century until the early 20th century and the foundations of some of the cottages can still be seen as well as the remains of an engine house and a restored, tall chimney. The mines were quite shallow and included early 'bell' pits but there was always a problem with water and the history of the site shows the constant difficulties faced in obtaining adequate pumping equipment that ranged from wind-powered pumps to waterwheel-powered pumps and, later, steam-powered pumps.[58] Grid Ref. NT97083772 (centre).

Beyond Ford Moss to the south-east, is the rock-art site at Roughting Linn which has public access from a minor road between Kimmerston and the B6525 road. It is said that Roughting Linn is named after a nearby waterfall from 'linn' meaning a pool and 'roughting' meaning a bellowing noise. The rock-art is of the cup and

Cup with circular grooved rings, groove running from it and 'sunburst' above.

ring type of which there are many, varied examples that cover a large exposed area of fell sandstone. This is a site of major significance and it is a pity that it has not received any protection from weather and visitor erosion although perhaps its hidden location gives some protection against the latter. The site was discovered in 1852 by William Greenwell who reported it to the Archaeological Institute in Newcastle; sadly, it was not formally recorded and written up. George Tate did some drawings in the mid 19th century and there have been a number of detailed surveys since then. A great deal has been written about the styles found in cup and ring markings and much speculation on the age and purpose of rock-art found in Northumberland. The carvings are thought to be of Neolithic and Bronze Age origin.[59]

To the west of the rock-art slabs is an Iron Age hill fort or camp that stands on the edge of a steep drop. On the east side, where there is no natural slope, there are at least five ramparts.[60] The rock-art site and the Iron Age fort are Scheduled Ancient Monuments and, with regard to protection, English Heritage has listed the camp on the *At Risk Register* with the condition shown as 'generally unsatisfactory with major localized problems' and with the trend as 'declining'.[61]

Back at Ford Bridge, the second of the Ford & Etal Estate's main fishing beats runs for over a mile upstream with twelve pools making up the beat, some of them stretching for 200 to 300 yards with the water running at a slower pace than other parts of the river.

I have not really strayed too far from Ford Bridge and the R. Till but, if I have, I am glad that I did so; the previous paragraph brings me back from my wanderings.

7

Ford Bridge to Tweed

Less than one mile downstream from Ford Bridge is the Ford Forge Mill, as it is described on the modern OS map. This is the former hamlet of Ford Forge mentioned in the last chapter. Eneas Mackenzie's description in 1825 of the plating forge echoes the description in 1778/9 by W. Hutchinson who also emphasizes Lady Delaval's benevolence towards the family's tenants and estate workers and her influence on Sir John Hussey Delaval's improvements to his lands. Hutchinson believed that she 'was a chief cause of the Iron Manufactury carried on near Ford being brought to its present significance'.[1]

Hutchinson describes the situation of the forge as 'romantic and the whole scene picturesque'. In 1779, the forge hammers were powered by water wheels supplied by water from a dam and a 'fine canal, from whence it breaks over the wear [sic] in a beautiful cascade; and being intercepted in its lower course by rocks and hillocks, divides into several streams'. Hutchinson's descriptions (which also include the scenery in the background and Cheviot, 'awfully supreme and majestic') are very much in tune with the start of the Romantic Era in British literature and art. The layout of the buildings in 1779 is still recognizable today from Hutchinson's description of them, 'The buildings for the forge, as you look up the river, lay to the left; on the opposite side is a water-corn-mill'.

The FORGE near FORD CASTLE

The engraving of John Bailey's sketch in 1779 shows the double-wheeled Heatherslaw corn mill on the right, facing Ford corn mill and the Ford Manor mill on the east bank with the new forge built in front. The dam wall can be seen curving across the Till. Reproduced from W. Hutchinson's *A View of Northumberland*. No copyright infringement.

In 1855, Ford Forge was part of Ford Constablewick (the jurisdiction of a local administrator and keeper of the peace) along with the village of Ford and the hamlets of Ford Bridge, Ford Common, Ford Mill, Ford Moss and Ford West Field. The buildings at Ford Forge accommodated the following businesses, A. E. Allan & Co., grocers, drapers and ironmongers; Thomas Black and Sons, spade, shovel and agricultural implement suppliers; Allan Mark & Sons. Joiners and cartwrights.[2] Ford Mill was the hamlet opposite the forge on the other (west) side of the Till and some workers from there

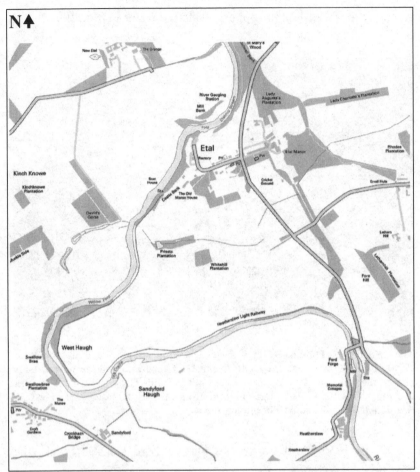

Ford Forge, Crookham and Etal. Distance from north to south. Distance from Crookham to Ford Bridge, about 1 mile. Contains Ordnance Survey data © Crown copyright and database right 2014.

crossed the river to work at the forge. For example, the 1841 census shows the Black and Tindle families living and working at Ford Forge with the male members of working age described as 'Blacksmiths' (Thomas Black, 53, the head of the firm, described as 'Merchant'); two male members of the Nesbit family, blacksmiths from Ford Mills, crossed the bridge each day to work at the forge. In 1851, Thomas

172

Black is described as a 'Toolmaker' with his birthplace being Scotland; the Nesbits are still working for him, with both the families having house servants by then, so their fortunes must have changed for the better. After 1782, the forge was reduced in size and the redundant areas together with the old mill were used for a fulling mill and dye house, leaving the grain milling to be concentrated on the Heatherslaw side of the river. In 1785, a joiner's shop was built, the forge enlarged to include an iron warehouse and other workshops were built along the river frontage. In about 1905, the buildings were converted into a sawmill and creosoting plant and the upper part of the original forge, which had become the house for the fuller, had been converted for use as a chapel with a house underneath.[3]

Some of the former forge buildings today with the entrance gates and yard of the Heatherslaw Light Railway (see p. 178).

In the photograph above, the building on the left was an iron warehouse and finishing shop and the building beyond it is the oldest part of the forge complex. The building in the distance was probably the joiner's shop. Out of the picture to the left, the new car park was once the tenter field for the fulling mill.

The reference to a chapel is interesting and presumably refers to a Baptist chapel that had been established at Ford Forge, long before 1905, in 1804. David Douglas in his 1846 *History of the Baptist Churches in the North of England*, refers to the Scottish Mission established in 1796 which, apart from conducting missions in foreign lands, also diffused its principles through England and Northern Ireland. Douglas says:

> A church was formed at Forge Ford...under the auspices of Mr. John Black, the owner of the Forge for the manufactory of spades etc. at this place. Mr. Alexander Kirkwood, now of Berwick, was ordained as pastor in 1804.[4]

As a result of an examination into the subject of baptism that had taken place in Edinburgh, it seems that a 'profession of faith' had been circulated amongst the churches in Scotland, England and Ireland. This included Ford Forge where it was said:

> Mr. Kirkwood and six or seven of the members of the church there were baptized. The others withdrew; and a new Baptist church [the Haldane church named after the chief Edinburgh proponent] was formed of twelve members. In 1807, Mr. Kirkwood removed to Beverley; and, in the meantime, the new church at Ford Forge was placed under the care of Mr. John Black, Junior, and Mr. William Dodds, who were set apart to the eldership by the late Mr. Archibald Maclean of Edinburgh.[5]

174

As the Black family had originated in Scotland they may have been particularly receptive to the new Baptist thinking that had come out of Edinburgh.

Douglas says that, in 1844, a Baptist chapel had been recently built that had several preaching stations. Thomas Black, the youngest son of John Black, was the pastor after his two elder brothers John (junior, mentioned above) and Robert had both assumed the position but had died in 1807 and 1809.[6] G. A Catherall says that the Forge Ford chapel 'came from the same source as the church at Wooler' and that there was some resentment in the area, particularly amongst Presbyterians, against the 'Scotch Baptists'.[7]

It must have been difficult to maintain the independence of a small church but, in 1883, it is recorded that the Berwick church 'appealed for assistance for a minister to be stationed at or near Berwick to be engaged in evangelistic work in the North of Northumberland, and Ford Forge'. In 1887, the church was accepted into the Northern Baptist Association and a pastor appointed to Ford Forge; pastoral work continued for several years but there were difficulties because of movement of population and although there is evidence that some activities continued until 1914, an attempt to revive the congregation in 1920 did not succeed.

To the west of Ford Forge, the OS map shows Heatherslaw and Old Heatherslaw. Old documents from the 13th century to the early 19th century refer to a medieval village at Old Heatherslaw but there are no surviving traces.[8] Wilfred Warren has written about the flexibility of the administrative system during the reign of Henry II when the king could avoid the necessity of using the judicial process through the courts and merely order that a wrong should be put right. He uses Heatherslaw as an example when a dispute arose between the monks of Durham and the Muschamp(e) family. The barony was in the hands of Cecily de Muschamp(e) and her son who then denied the right of the monks to hold the manor of Heatherslaw because they could not produce a charter. The monks complained to the king who issued a writ commanding Cecily and her son to grant the manor to the monks on the strength of inquiries amongst those who had seen the monks seised of the manor by Thomas Muschamp(e) senior. The Muschamps did not comply and the king had to intervene again:

> I am astonished and greatly displeased that you have not done what I ordered in my writs...Now, however, I firmly order you on pain of forfeiture to execute my commands without further delay, so that I hear no further complaint about it for want of full right.

Witness, Reginald earl of Cornwall. At Northampton.[9]

The Rev. Hastings Neville, one time Rector of Ford, describes in 1896, how Heatherslaw must have been much larger in the past with cottages on both sides of the street, like Etal. Like Ford and Etal, Heatherslaw was described as a 'town' although perhaps not as large as they were. In Neville's time, the garden still remained of the former manor house and he refers to a field to the east of the remaining single row of cottages called the Chapel Field in which ploughing sometimes disturbed the foundations of what could have been a chantry, perhaps reflecting the hamlet's religious connection with the monks of Durham.[10] The Rev. Neville refers to the village stocks and to a pump and a well that was so nearly the scene of a tragedy one Christmas Day when a six year old girl fell down the well having leant over the side opposite her mother, who was letting down the bucket. The mother rushed to the nearest house and, fortunately, a young blacksmith came and slid down the chain to rescue the girl who was clinging to a beam.[11] Mawer suggests that the name 'Heatherslaw' may derive from *Hæðhere's* hill although the full word does not appear in OE. It may just mean 'Heather-hill'.[12]

Heatherslaw Bridge or Ford Forge Bridge from the Heatherslaw Mill side, showing the steel plate decking (now covered). The Grid Ref. is NT93323847.

The present bridge across the Till that links the former forge side of the river with the restored Heatherslaw Mill was built in 1877 by A. & J. Main & Co. of Glasgow. It is listed Grade II and is built of cast iron, steel and rock-faced stone with large, corniced end-piers and mid-point piers. It has steel, trellis parapets with a 12 feet wide roadway supported on large, iron beams. Until 2013, the road surface was made from war surplus, perforated, iron strips. These have since been covered or replaced by a non-slip material in two colours to separate pedestrians from vehicles.[13] Nearby, alder, sycamore, horse chestnut, poplar and willow may be seen on the river banks.

The former Ford Forge works is now home to the 15 inch gauge Heatherslaw Light Railway (the most northerly steam railway in England) which was established in 1989 with an original $1\frac{1}{4}$ miles of track between Heatherslaw and Etal that was increased to $2\frac{1}{4}$ miles in 2004. The railway is and was the work of enthusiasts who responded to the late Lord Joicey's wish for a project that would enhance the visitor attractions on the Ford & Etal Estates. Much of the building, refurbishment and repairs to the steam and diesel locomotives and carriages is done by the enthusiasts at the Heatherslaw workshops; there is also ongoing maintenance of the stations, platforms and track.[14]

The Heatherslaw Light Railway steam engine 'Bunty' pulling carriages at the passing place, having left the terminus at Etal on the return to Heatherslaw.

There was a big set-back in 2008 when flood water and mud from the R. Till covered the railway, the ticket office, other buildings, locomotives and carriages and washed away part of the track, but much hard work enabled the railway to be back in service within months. The narrow gauge railway takes visitors in partly enclosed, partly glazed carriages from Heatherslaw to Etal Castle and return, around the loop of Letham Hill Haugh giving opportunities to spot wildlife along a tranquil stretch of the R. Till.

Looking down on the R. Till and over the fields of Letham Hill Haugh (or West Haugh) is the village of Crookham. The haugh lies within what must be the largest meander of the river along the whole of its length, this crook giving its name to the village, *crucum* in the 13th century, perhaps from the Anglo-Saxon, *cruc* and *ham* meaning a settlement on the bend of a river. Writing in 1828, William Parson and William White describe the village:

> CROOKHAM, OR CRECUM, a village and constablewick…It consists principally of one street of 44 houses, a good School, and a Presbyterian Chapel, the latter of which was erected in 1745, will seat 1500 persons, and is now under the ministry of the Rev. Thomas Hall, who has officiated here more than eighteen years. This constablewick includes the whole of the Pallinsburn estate, and Crookham, and Barelees, which belong to the Ford estate. In January, 1828, it contained 99 houses, and 478 inhabitants.[15]

Crookham was, at one time, within the same barony as Ford and owned by the Muschamps before passing to the Herons and then to the Carrs. It was only when the Carrs lost their claim to Ford that

Crookham started to be become a separate entity. In 1663, Thomas Carr of Belford relinquished his claim on Ford in return for the land and farm at Marden Demesne in Crookham, conveyed to him in tail male (a line of inheritance restricted to males). This consisted of 16 stints or cowgates (a feudal term granting pasture rights for a fixed number of animals) and three cottages at Crookham. Another part of Crookham became separated as a result of a mortgage taken by Thomas Carr from Ralph Bradford who was given possession of $8^{1}/_{2}$ farms pending repayment of the capital by 1664; failure to repay would convert possession to ownership. The money was not repaid and the land went to the Bradford heirs before being sold to John Jenkins of Gateshead. Barelees Farm remained with the Ford Estate.

The Jenkins land was sold twice, firstly in 1735 and then in 1763 to Adam Askew of Heatherslaw. The Marden Demesne land was first sold by the descendants of Thomas Carr and then passed through three subsequent ownerships ending up with George Adam Askew in 1813. The united property was named Pallinsburn. Adam Askew then sold Heatherslaw and ten cottages in Crookham to Sir John Hussey Delaval and in return bought 200 acres at Crookham West Field and two acres of a field called Southfield or Award Bree together with all the tithes.

At this time (the late 18th century), there were two parts to Crookham; the Ford estate owned the village of Crookham, Crookham Demesne to the north-east of the village, Barelees to the north-west and Crookham Ridge on the south, all of which eventually passed to the Marquess of Waterford and then, in the early 20th century), to Lord Joicey. The second part, Pallinsburn estate, consisted of Pallinsburn House and land, extending to 240 acres, together with Pallinsburn East and West Farms and Burn Farm. The estate passed down through the Askew family until it was sold in 1911 to Major Mitchell.[16] The property, amounting to 1,500 acres, was sold by the descendants of Major Mitchell in 2004. The name, 'Pallinsburn', is said to come from Paulinus, the Archbishop of York who preached, converted and baptized people in the area. The baptismal lake is said to have given rise to the name of the burn, Paulinus' Burn or 'Pallinsburn' that flows into the Till at Crookham.

Historically, Crookham village has been described as 'always having been a modest sized village' and this is confirmed by the figure of 24 men from the village eligible for military service in 1762.[17] The Parson and White Trade Directory for 1828 gives a variety of occupations for the village (including Pallinsburn); schoolmaster, Presbyterian minister, four joiners (one also an auctioneer), millwright, two mole catchers, baker, sadler, violin maker, three innkeepers (one also a farrier), two blacksmiths, three farmers (Marden, Crookham Westfield and Crookham Eastfield), two gardeners, three grocers (one also a draper), two shoemakers and three tailors, as well as Mr. Askew of Pallinsburn and his agent.[18]

Kelly's Trade Directory of 1910 states that the former National School had become disused for school purposes and was being used for Divine service on Sunday afternoons by the Church of England rector of Ford. This would have been the 'new school' that had been built in 1856 capable of holding 120 children but with an average attendance of 44 children.[19] In 1910, there was a combined shop and post office and this remained in place until fairly recent times.

From the 17th century onwards, the village church was Presbyterian. In 1662, nearly 2,000 dissenting clergymen were ejected from the Church of England for refusing to abide by the provisions of the Act of Uniformity that required them to use the revised Book of Common Prayer in all services and to assent to the 39 articles of faith. As a result, dissenting congregations were formed consisting of independents, Presbyterians or Baptists. These congregations were persecuted and subject to severe legal penalties to prevent their activities; this meant that they could only survive by meeting in secret. After 1689, their activities were tolerated but restrictions were only finally removed in the mid 19th century. Presbyterianism had several branches and many churches in Northumberland often had Scottish or English in their title to denote their origins.

In 1697, a Presbyterian church was founded at Etal and, in 1732, a group from Etal founded a church in Crookham, meeting in non purpose-built premises. A dedicated church was built in 1745 and the present church was built in 1932. In 1949, the Etal church combined with Crookham and, in 1972, Presbyterians and Congregationalists in England combined to form the United Reform Church. The fact that there were Presbyterian churches in north Northumberland, close to Scotland reflects the strong cross-border contacts and also movement of population. Many people in north Northumberland have Scottish roots and economic factors would have had a major influence with a southward drift of population in search of work and a better life during times of hardship north of the border.

P. Anderson Graham in *Highways and Byways in Northumbria*, 1921, describes Crookham as 'standing high on jutting ground...looking across Till to the Etal Haughs, and with Flodden and the blue Cheviot range in the opposite direction'.[20] It is true that when the village is viewed from across the Till from near Etal, its raised position is quite obvious, almost like an island in the surrounding countryside. In 1921, the previous Presbyterian meeting-house was just 'plain, square slated'. Graham refers to the appearance of the village during the early years of Lady Waterford when many of the 'gaun folk' (active people going about their business) 'lived in houses thatched down to the ground, and each cottage had a midden at the door'. Today, Crookham is an attractive village with a United Reform church and a village hall. Like many rural communities, it no longer has a school or a shop or a post office but, like other villages in north Northumberland that I have visited on my journey, it has a strong community spirit and retains an identity of its own.

Crookham and the farm of Sandyford (see map on p. 172) were both ancient crossing points of the R. Till and the Pallinsburn respectively. Travellers could cross the Till perhaps at the Willow Ford which is marked on the modern OS map where the 'crook' bends round to the north-east after passing below the village. Sandyford, by its name, was a ford across the Pallinsburn just before it enters the Till. These fords were possibly used by the English army before the Battle of Flodden, but there has been much conjecture about this. Whereas the vanguard of the army crossed the Till lower down at Twizel Bridge, the crossing point or points for the remainder of the army might have been at Heaton Mill ford about a mile south of

Twizel Bridge. Did any part of the army cross the Till at Crookham or the Pallinsburn at Sandyford? English Heritage's Battlefield Report quotes Edward Hall's *Chronicle* published in 1548:

> Then, when the Englishmen had passed a little brook [Pallinsburn], called Sandyford, which is but a man's step over, and that the smoke was passed [a smokescreen generated by the Scottish army], and the air fair and clear, each army might plainly see one another at hand'.[21]

The other possible crossing point for the English army over the Pallinsburn would have been at Branx Brig, north-east of Branxton village, below Windy Law. These are unresolved questions but perhaps archaeology may one day provide some answers.

The 'crook' or loop in the R. Till below Crookham which is on the higher ground to the left. Willow Ford is around the far bend of the river to the right.

The large, westward loop in the course of the river below Crookham is very marked and, in 1922, Kenneth Vickers suggested that this was evidence of the R. Till trying to re-establish its former pre-glacial route towards its junction with the Tweed at Cornhill. He remarked on a corresponding eastward loop of the Tweed at Cornhill, as this river also tries to re-establish its old valley. The line between Cornhill and Crookham would have been the lower limit of the lake that was formed as the Tweed glacier receded and dropped its glacial deposits along the length of the old valley. As the ice melted back into the Tweed valley, the overflow from the lake would have flowed over the glacial drift and carved out a new channel for the Till into the Carboniferous rock along its present route.[22] The land within the 'crook' is flat and was used for horse races in 1824, but discontinued the following year 'for want of sufficient encouragement'.[23]

P. Anderson Graham remarked on the different character of the vegetation along the banks of the river below Crookham before the character of the river changes lower down, at Etal. Here, the stiller waters along the margins grow sedges or 'segs' with rushes here and there. Graham said that, in the old days, willows were planted on the banks for harvesting the wands to use with straw for making beehives, baskets and the long baskets called 'swills' for collecting potatoes and turnips. He thought that the name, 'Willow Ford', at Crookham, was as old as the battle of Flodden; the willows were neglected now (1921) but looked more picturesque in their untended state.[24]

I was on my own when walking along the bank here and, because I was not making conversation, I was very fortunate to see an otter gliding down the river sideways with his/her head facing me and making loud, snuffling noises; I am not sure whether this was a noise of pleasure or whether the otter was sniffing the air to catch a scent. I was spotted as soon as I reached for my camera and the animal dived under water. However, I had sufficient time to be able to identify that it was an otter and not a mink. An easy way to distinguish one from the other is that an otter swims with its body beneath the surface and its head out of the water and its tail pointing upwards whereas the body of a mink is visible above the surface.

The European otter, *Lutra lutra*, is native to the R. Tweed and its tributaries. In the past, the otter population in the United Kingdom suffered from persecution, loss of habitat, depleted fish stocks and the use of insecticides until it had diminished to such an extent that strong concentrations were only to be found in Scotland, particularly the north and west and part of the Borders. Otters also survived in parts of Wales and in Ireland. Fortunately, there has been a recovery in numbers and, because of improvements in water quality giving rise to more sustainable fish populations in rivers, otters are now to be found throughout the United Kingdom and Ireland.

An otter usually lives for three or four years but this can be longer and a male inhabits a range of 25 miles or more (with the female about half this), feeding mainly on a variety of fish species but also small mammals and birds, depending on availability at the time. In England and Wales, otters are protected under the Conservation of Habitats and Species Regulations 2010 that consolidate all the amendments made to earlier regulations dating from 1994.

It is illegal to:

* deliberately capture, injure or kill an otter;

* deliberately disturb an otter in such a way as to be likely to significantly affect the local distribution or abundance of otters or the ability of any significant group of otters to survive, breed, rear or nurture their young;

* damage or destroy an otter holt;

* possess or transport an otter or any part of an otter;

* sell (or offer for sale) or exchange an otter.

Under Section 9(4)(b) and (c) and (5) of the Wildlife and Countryside Act 1981 (as amended), it is also illegal to:

* intentionally or recklessly disturb any otter whilst it is occupying a holt;

* intentionally or recklessly obstruct access to a holt.

The presence of otters in the R. Tweed catchment is a contributory reason for the catchment's selection as a Special Area of Conservation (SAC) under Article 3 of the European Commission's Habitat Directive. The R. Tweed SAC is part of a European network of high-quality conservation sites that will make a significant contribution to conserving the 189 habitat types and 788 species (the otter is one) identified in Annexes I and II of the Directive (as amended).

From Crookham, the R. Till flows on to Etal, passing below the formidable castle ruins that stand high above the river. There are several historic sites before reaching the castle; looking at the map on p. 172, there is an oval shaped area between David's Gorse and the river that is the site of a medieval village at Etal. This would have been the village of New Etal which The Northumberland County History Committee in its 1922 *History of Northumberland* said was burnt by the Scots in 1533 and shown in a survey of 1541 to have been quite separate from Etal Castle. Its position on the other side of the river from the castle is recorded in the survey:

> The towneshippe of new Etayle conteyneth viii husband lands plenyshed without fortresse or barmekyn and ys of thinherytaunce of the Erl of Rutland, and the tenants thereof in tyme of need resorte to his castell of Etayle standynge upon the Est side of the said river of Tyll [25]

Also, on the bend of the river, between David's Gorse and Priest's Plantation, there is the site of a medieval, stone bridge, the foundation remains of which are said to be still visible when the river is running low.[26] It was over this bridge, 'the brigge at Etayle' that the captured Scottish guns were brought to Etal Castle after the Battle of Flodden in 1513. The bridge, which connected the east bank with New Etal, collapsed in 1541 and Graham says that Sir George Bowes (1527-1580), one-time Marshal of Berwick and escort to Mary, Queen of Scots on her journey from Carlisle to Bolton Castle, lamented its decay on the grounds that it 'afforded ready passage when the river Tyll is waxen greate and past the rydinge upon horseback'. Bowes asked that it be 're-edified' but despite this request being repeated several times during the following centuries, nothing was done.[27]

There was certainly a bridge (probably timber) in the 18th century that, according to William Parson and William White, writing in 1828:

> was swept away in a great flood more than 50 years ago, since which disaster a ferry-boat has been stationed here, but it is hoped that in this age of improvement, a new bridge will

soon be erected for the better accommodation of the inhabitants.[28]

This bridge was not replaced either; it was located further downstream from the stone bridge below the castle walls. This was the site of the ferry referred to above as well as a boat house; both were still in place in the 1930s when the small boat was pulled across the Till by ropes attached to the bow and stern.

The modern OS map shows 'Lookout' and 'Lookout Plantation' on the top of high ground to the west of the ferry and west of the castle on the opposite bank. This used to be the hamlet of 'Keek Out' which was the spot used to keep a watch to see whether the Scots were coming to raid the village.

In 1250, the manor of Etal was held by Robert Manners as a tenant of Robert Muschamp. The Manners family occupied the castle until the 15th century but, earlier in the same century, there was an ongoing feud between the Manners and their neighbours, the Herons of Ford Castle. William Heron attacked Etal Castle but was killed in the assault and Hastings Neville tells us that:

> The whole Country was divided into two hostile factions in consequence of this fray, till ultimately by the arbitration of the priors of Durham and Tynemouth, Manners agreed to have 500 masses said for Heron's soul and to pay an annuity to his widow.[29]

The Manners family ceased to use the castle as their main residence at the end of the 15th century and it was leased to the Collingwoods under a lease of three lives. The Collingwoods were constables of the castle when it was captured and battered down by

James IV of Scotland, before the Battle of Flodden. As mentioned, the ruined castle was used to store the captured Scottish cannon that must have been pulled to Etal by teams of (perhaps captured) oxen.

The keep of Etal Castle stands high above the east bank of the R. Till and, originally, would not have been obscured by vegetation as it is today.

The keep of Etal Castle is now just a shell but the outlines of the various floors can be clearly seen internally, starting with the tunnel-vaulted basement, the ground floor that was probably the kitchen with its large fireplace, the first floor that was probably the Great Hall and the upper floors that were sleeping quarters. The large, imposing gatehouse is a prominent site at the west end of the village and, at one time, the castle would have had a moat and a drawbridge. Also, because of a doorway that can be seen in the wall at first floor

190

level and projecting stones either side of the arch, the gatehouse probably had some form of timber defensive structure in front of it.

The worn Manners family shield is above the gatehouse arch and there is a replacement portcullis with recesses within the arch to allow four defensive beams to be slotted into place when required. In front of and on each side of the arch, there are two cannons from HMS *Royal George* that foundered at Spithead in 1782 with the loss of between 900 and 1200 officers and men. Many items were salvaged from the wreck and some were offered for sale. The cannon were put there by Lord Frederick FitzClarence in the 19th century. Etal Castle was passed to the state in 1975 and is cared for by English Heritage. It is a Grade I listed building.[30]

The present English Heritage visitor centre for the castle is housed in the former Presbyterian meeting-house and is a Grade II listed building. The congregation was formed towards the end of the 17th century and the building dates from about 1703 but was largely rebuilt around 1800. It was used as a joiner's workshop before its present use.[31]

By 1547, Thomas Manners, as Earl of Rutland, passed Etal estate to the Crown in exchange for other property. Some time after 1567, the estate passed to Sir Robert Carr on whose death it was under sequestration by Parliament for eleven and a half years during the Civil War, before being restored to William Carr on his paying a sum of £539 8s. 7d. in 1653. It was his descendant, Sir William Carr, who built Etal manor house in 1748.

Sir William's daughter, Isabella, married James, Earl of Errol whose daughter, Lady Charlotte Hay, succeeded to the estate in 1798.

She married the Rev. William Holwell and, with the king's permission, took the name, Carr, becoming Lady Charlotte Holwell Carr. Because her brother inherited the title, Earl of Errol, he was prevented from inheriting the estate under the terms of his grandfather's will, but Charlotte, in order to prevent litigation, consented to divide the Etal rents with her brother. On her death in 1800, her infant son inherited the estate causing the Earl to commence an unsuccessful legal action because the guardians had thought it inappropriate to pay any proportion of the rents to the Earl.

The infant, William Holwell Carr was confirmed in his inheritance of the estate, but died when only seven years old and the estate devolved on his aunt, the Countess of Glasgow, the wife of George Boyle, 4th Earl of Glasgow. In 1821, their daughter, Lady Augusta Boyle, married Lord Frederick FitzClarence, one of ten illegitimate children of William IV and the actress, Mrs. Jordan.[32]

To the east of Etal Castle is the attractive village of Etal with its thatched and slate-roofed estate cottages mostly set back on both sides of the street and with the buildings separated from the street by cottage gardens. I always admire the chunky, graduated slates on the roof of the village hall and other properties. There is a public house, a village shop with café and post office and a village hall. The attraction of the gardens and setting of the village today was the same in 1841 when the Rev. Dr. Gilly of Norham wrote:

> To see what a village in our northern regions may be, and ought to be, go to Etall. There you will find flower-gardens in perfection, with the village-green as smooth as a lawn in the best kept pleasure-ground, and the rustic benches under the

spreading branches and sycamore. One fine tree, with a seat around its trunk, is conspicuous, with an inscription which shows the considerate kindness of the noble family [Lord Frederick & Lady Augusta FitzClarence] now residing in the mansion-house, 'Willie Wallace's tree'. I believe the old man is still alive in whose honour the tree is thus devoted to longevity.[33]

Although Dr. Gilly's description resonates with the appearance of Etal today, the cottages were rebuilt by Lord Joicey in the early 20th century. However, their character was retained and both Ford and Etal villages are now attractive, model villages although quite different in appearance.

At the road junction to the east of the village, a drive leads up to Etal Manor. This is an attractive country house of ashlar masonry and Scottish slate which, as mentioned, was built in 1748 for William Carr. Etal Manor was enlarged by William Carr in 1767 and extended at the rear for James Laing in 1888; he purchased the estate after the death of Lady Augusta FitzClarence in 1876 and lived there until his death in 1901.

The particulars of sale for the auction on 2nd July 1885 at Tokenhouse Yard, Bank of England, show that the estate comprised 'The Residence'; farms at New Etal, Litham Hill, Watchlaw, Berry Hill, Rhodes Hill and Hay; The 'Black Bull' Inn; numerous houses, gardens etc. comprising the village of Etal including the remains of Etal Castle; several enclosures of accommodation land; Etal Moor Colliery and shooting and fishing, all amounting to 3,437 acres, 4 roods, 38 perches.[34] Sir James Laing (1823-1901, knighted 1897) was the head of Sunderland shipbuilders, James Laing and Sons Limited. James Laing divided the property between his three sons and, in 1908, they sold the estate to the 1st Lord Joicey.

Etal Manor, which is a Grade II* listed building, is a private, family home and is not open to visitors.[35] A short distance east of the house, within the private policies, is a tapering, rectangular, sandstone block on a square, moulded base. It is listed Grade II.[36] There is an inscription from 1850, stating:

> As an humble mark of gratitude to providence for happiness passed on these estates during a period of thirty-two years. Frederick FitzClarence had this inscription made on leaving for India.

Beneath this, in a moulded panel, is inscribed:

> As a tribute of thankfulness to the bounteous giver of all good for unnumbered mercies during his life James Laing inscribed this on his 70th birthday.

The Church of St. Mary the Virgin, on the right hand side of the drive, is open to visitors. It is a Grade II listed building designed in 1858 by William Butterfield for Lady FitzClarence. It is built of pink, sandstone ashlar with dressings and bands of beige sandstone with graduated Lakeland slates.[37] Lady FitzClarence built the church as a burial place for her husband, Lord Frederick, who died in 1853 at Poona in India while he was Commander-in-Chief of the Indian Army. Lord Frederick, Lady Augusta and their daughter, Augusta and Lord Frederick's aide-de-camp, are buried in the south aisle of the church. The church was built as a Chapel-of-Ease, normally a building situated within a parish for those who could not easily reach the parish church; in this case the church was a private, family chapel and had a chaplain but no parish because Etal village was in the parish of Ford. From the 1920s, the Rector of Ford was also Chaplain of St. Mary's and, in the 1970s in order to regularize the position, St. Mary's was transferred from Ford & Etal Estates to the parish of Ford, which was renamed Ford & Etal parish.

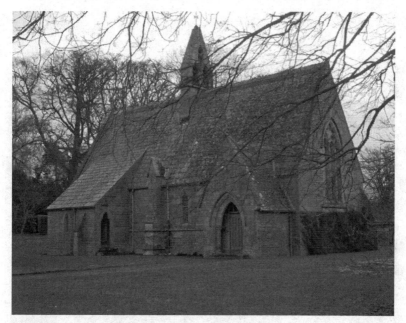

Church of St. Mary the Virgin, Etal.

Downstream from Etal Castle, the R. Till passes over a weir and a ford (Grid Ref. NT92573955). The ford is marked on the map on p. 172; the weir is just on the upstream side of it. The word 'weir' comes from the Anglo-Saxon *wer*, one meaning of which is a device to trap fish. Weirs can be built for a number of reasons such as trapping fish, flow management, river stabilization or channelling water to a mill. The weir at Etal was built to direct water towards a sluice and channel supplying a corn mill on the south bank, above the ford. The first edition of the OS 25 ins. to 1 mile map of 1860 shows the weir and, below it, a building, clearly labelled Corn Mill, projecting into the river. However, by 1897, the map does not show a corn mill and the third edition, in 1920, although showing a sluice and a channel passing underneath a building, probably depicts a water-driven power-house for the village.

The ford at Etal seen from the north bank, with the weir in the distance.

P. Anderson Graham describes how the yeomen used to take their corn to be ground on the back of a packhorse, returning home with the meal less a fee or levy paid to the miller called the 'multure' (from Middle English, *multir*; Latin, *molitus*, adj: 'ground'). This was usually a proportion of the ground grain or of the flour made. Later, the meal was delivered by the 'poker', a term derived from 'pokes', as the bags or sacks were called then. Graham says that much cheating went on over the indefinite levy on the corn as described in Chaucer's 'The Reeve's Tale'.[37]

The ford at Etal, downstream from the weir, is very old. It now has a concrete surface but it must have been in existence for hundreds of years, perhaps even since Roman times. The river level is quite high with a fast-flowing current in the photograph on p. 196.

Downstream of the ford is the site of a suspension bridge that was in existence until comparatively recently. Tony Dickens, writing in 1975, says that it 'is quite an experience as it swings and sways above the river Till'.[38] It was quite narrow and was for pedestrian use only; it was the property of Lord Joicey. Dickens thought that the lack of a bridge at Etal was a good thing by not having traffic roaring across it heading north, thereby preserving the tranquility of the village of Etal. The stretch of river below the ford is known as Etalmill Stream. Mawer says that the name 'Etal' derives from the 'Haugh of Eata', *Eata* being a common Old Northumbrian name.[39]

The river now starts to swing round below the present New Etal farm and cottages in a more north-westerly direction, one which it maintains, subject to multi-directional meanders, all the way to its confluence with the Tweed at Tillmouth. Just before it does so and on the opposite (east) bank to New Etal, are the ruins of the chapel of the Blessed Virgin Mary. The chapel is thought to have been founded before 1345 and it must have been sited there because it is next to a well that was also dedicated to St. Mary. There is an outline of stones below the path and the water from the well has been piped and discharges within the rectangle formed by the stones. A stone cross was placed at the east end by Lady Augusta FitzClarence and, in recent years, this was rescued, repaired and re-erected by local people who found it lying broken on the ground. However, Hastings Neville tells us that the foundation of the old chapel cannot be seen now as it is underneath the path. It was once excavated and found to have been about 30 feet in length; the workmen found many skulls and bones.[40]

The outline of stones and the cross at St. Mary's Chapel, above the R. Till.

St. Mary's chapel was a Chantry Chapel that would have been established so that a Chantry Priest could sing a stated number of masses over a stipulated period for the soul of a deceased person; this was probably the owner of Etal manor at the time. Neville gives an

198

example of this as the 500 masses that were said for the soul of William Heron of Ford after he was killed when attacking Etal Castle, but it is not known where these took place. Neville also says that Lady Augusta had thought of building her new church on the site of the chapel and building a burial vault for her husband on the spot within the stones and marked by the cross.

A little further north on the same side of the river is the much-depleted ruin of Barley Mill and the miller's cottage. The ruin and the outfall to the river are much overgrown and the origin of the watermill is unknown. Most of the buildings have now gone but the whole mill is shown on the first edition of the OS map and a smaller section on the second edition map. It seems that the mill ceased production between 1861 and 1871 and many of the buildings were demolished or had fallen down by the 1890s.[41]

The path along the river from Etal past the chantry ruin and the mill ruin passes through the wooded area called Lady Augusta's Plantation which, when I was there in January, was carpeted in many places with snowdrops. The path drops down to the riverbank beyond the mill, giving a view of a weir that, at one time, crossed the width of the river but now only stretches across an area known as 'The Pool' which is a good sea trout 'hold'. Here, there is a carved, wooden seat and a notice board encouraging people to stand or sit quietly to see and hear the wildlife. There is a list of animals, birds and insects that can be seen, illustrated by excellent drawings done by children at Ford First School.

During my visit, the river was high, very brown and running fast, so not the best conditions for seeing herons gazing into the water or dippers that need raised stones to hold onto as they wade into the river. The path along the river is well-engineered and quite wide and Neville says that this is because it was once a carriage drive, constructed at great cost by Lord Frederick FitzClarence.[42]

The stretch of river below Etal is the third of the Ford & Etal Estates' main fishing beats, known as Upper Tindal. It runs for over 1½ miles with 16 pools. The Estate description states that this is where the nature of the Till changes, becoming much faster-flowing over rock with white water streams into deep pools, creating ideal fly water.[43] Beyond Barley Mill, the R. Till flows into the start of a large loop, beginning with the Short Stream and the Long Stream.

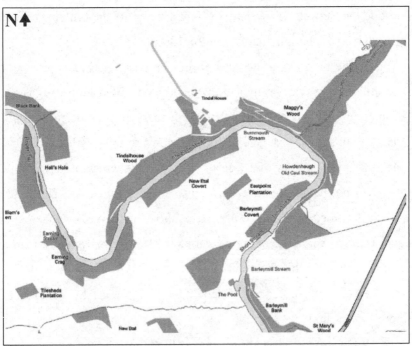

The R. Till north-west of Etal from Barley Mill to Black Bank. Distance across the map from west to east, about 1¼ miles. Contains Ordnance Survey data © Crown copyright and database right 2014.

R. Till turning into Short Stream with Long Stream beyond and Howdenheugh Old Caul Stream in the distance.

Howdenheugh Old Caul Stream (perhaps from 'caul', Scots for cold or perhaps 'cauld', Scots for a weir or dam) is on a bend of the loop before the entry of the Duddomill Burn from the north-east. The burn comes down from higher ground in the vicinity of Rhodes Hill and Etal Moor and the 1860 OS map shows Etal Colliery on the side of the burn with seven or more coal pits above it on the moor.

The colliery is said to have been working before 1819; its operators, who would have been lessees of the estate, included (according to Parson and White, writing in 1828) the firm of Carr, Grey and Co., and (according to Durham Mining Museum) the firm of Scremerston & Shoreswood Coal Company from 1870 until closure in about 1890.[44]

At this point, I have to make a diversion, but only a small one of under two miles to the north-east, because I cannot leave out the Duddo Stone Circle that stands in a prominent position in a field at Grid Ref. NT93054370 with good views to the north and west in the direction of the Scottish Border. It has been described as 'the Stonehenge of north Northumberland' but this accolade seems to be somewhat exaggerated. Nevertheless, it is an impressive structure even in its present, depleted condition. The OS map describes it as 'Four Stones' but there are now five standing stones of weathered sandstone, dating from the Neolithic Era.

Duddo Stone Circle showing the five remaining megaliths.

There were originally seven stones but, before 1852, two stones were lost from the north-west quadrant. Of the remaining five, one stone fell sometime during the 19th century and was pulled away to allow ploughing across the interior of the circle but was re-erected in about 1903. Excavations in the 1890s revealed the socket holes for the missing stones and cremated, human remains were found within a central pit. Excavations in the 1980s re-established the positions of the two missing stones and radiocarbon dating of charcoal packing around the northernmost stone showed that the circle had been built around 2000 BC. A fragment of human bone from the central pit was dated to between 1740 and 1660 BC, suggesting that the burial was a later use of the site.

The stones vary in height between 1.5 m. and 2.3 m., with the largest stone being 1.8 m. wide and 0.5 m. in depth, all forming a circle of ten metres. One or more of the stones may have cup marks but some of these may be natural and it is difficult to be certain because of the deep weathering of the sandstone. The weathering has formed deep, vertical grooves, giving a very distinctive appearance.

One local name is 'The Singing Stones' due, it is thought, to the sound made by the wind as it whistles through them, the sound perhaps being amplified by the vertical grooves. The stones are also known as 'The Women' perhaps because of their 'waisted' look due to them being broader at the top than at ground level. The stones are listed as a Scheduled Ancient Monument under the Ancient Monuments and Archaeological Areas Act 1979, as amended.[45]

The Duddo Stone Circle with all its seven stones must have been passed or, at the very least, seen, by the English army on its march from Barmoor before crossing the R. Till on the eve of the Battle of Flodden. This was one of the thoughts in my mind when I was there with my companion on a warm, summer's day, although the photograph shows the approach of some threatening clouds.

The small village of Duddo is under a mile to the south-east of the stone circle. In medieval times, there was a village sited slightly to the west of the present village centre that was part of the Bishop of Durham's estate of Norhamshire. In the 16th century, a survey recorded eight husbandlands and, in the 18th century, there were 40 houses. William Parson and William White, writing in 1828, describe it as, 'a small township, consisting of two farms, a few cottages, and a colliery…On the rocky summit of Grindon Rigg, in this township, are the ruins of Duddo Tower…'[46] By 1855, there was also a chapel-of-ease and a public house and the population at that time (1851) was 286 people.[47]

The chapel-of-ease was a curacy attached to the vicarage of Norham and known as St. James the Great. It was built in 1832 but was converted to a school with an attached schoolhouse, supported by the lord of the manor, Thomas Friar. The building is Grade II listed and is now a private house.[48] The replacement parish church of All Saints was built in 1879, a little way out of the village and partly modelled on the Church of St. Mary on Holy Island, but this has also ceased to be a church and now has residential use whilst retaining its Grade II listing.[49] Duddo House, another Grade II listed building, was built between 1832 and 1830 and remains in private ownership.[50]

To the south-east is the ruin of the Grade II listed Duddo Tower. The remaining wall stands on the site of an earlier tower that was destroyed by James IV of Scotland on his foray into England in support of Perkin Warbeck, a claimant to the English throne. The wall is part of the rebuilt tower and much later; the tower was a simple rectangle with a projecting entrance wing on the south side.[51] Robert

Hugill in his *Borderland Castles & Peles*, describes the tower as something of a mystery because of its identity. On the one hand, the old tower may have been the stronghold of the Lords of Tillmouth but the style (or what remains of it) of the present building suggests that it may have been built after the Union of Scotland and England. [52]

Like many Northumberland villages, Duddo had its own tileworks and, like Etal, it also had a colliery, first sunk in 1832 and said to be one of the deepest mines in north Northumberland. It was known as the Greenlaw Walls Company when it was operated by Johnson & Carr but its name was changed to Duddo Colliery when it was operated by the Scremerston & Shoreswood Company. The pit was located behind Pit Cottage on the B6354 road, north of the village and comprised a number of worked seams, many of them workings belonging to the earliest pits and unknown to the miners. It was this that caused the pit disaster of April, 1857 when five men (two from the same family) were drowned when water broke through from an old pit and inundated the mine. The mine seems to have ceased production then or shortly thereafter.[53]

There was a decline in the population of Duddo village to 151 people in 1901. In the 20th century, a small group of council houses was built in the village and, today, the Duddo Community describes itself as a peaceful rural parish comprising the scattered hamlets of Duddo, Felkington, Grievestead, Grindon, Grindon Rigg, Shellacres, Tiptoe and Twizel. It highlights the ageing population and the difficulties faced by rural communities in Northumberland but also emphasizes the advantages that accrue from the magnificent countryside, the proximity of the Heritage Coast and the

Northumberland National Park.[54] Allen Mawer says that the name 'Duddo' derives from 'Duda's *hoh* (OE for a promontory).[55]

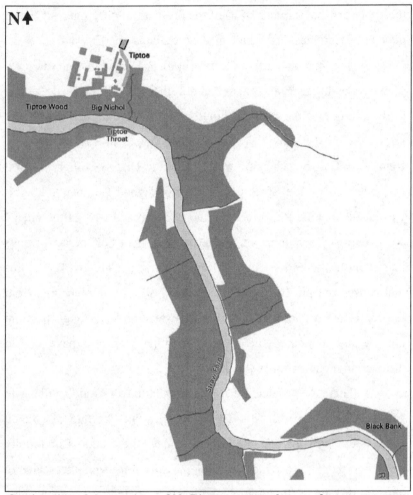

Continuation of the map on p. 200. Distance across the map from west to east, about 1 mile. Contains Ordnance Survey data © Crown copyright and database right 2014.

I am back from my detour, but it wasn't very far and well worth doing. The R. Till flows on from Duddomill Burn and Tindal

House and the last of Ford & Etal's main fishing beats at Lower Tindal where there is a two miles or more stretch of river in a deep gorge with many, white water streams over rock into deep pools. The estate describes it as 'a beat for the able-bodied but well worth it'. The river sweeps past Hell Hole and Black Bank on the east bank and King William's Covert on the west bank, the latter surely a tribute from Lord Frederick FitzClarence to his father. In 2006, Tiptoe Farm was awarded the title of 'Most Beautiful Farm in Britain' and is a LEAF (Linking Environment and Farming) Demonstration Farm, growing top quality crops (particularly, heritage potatoes) with care for the environment and wildlife. Tiptoe farmhouse is a mid 18th century building with early 19th century additions and is a Grade II listed building.[56]

In the report on the meeting of The Berwickshire Naturalists Club in July 1860, it was noted that:

> the long drive made by the late Lord Frederick FitzClarence along its [the Till's] banks, cut out of the slopes and through the woodland glades...is continued a long way down the river, by the romantic rocks of Tipthoe [sic] and Tindal House, now called Clarence Dale.[57]

When I was walking along here by myself, the atmosphere seemed timeless and I half expected to see a carriage coming towards me; it made me reflect on the poet Edward Thomas's suggestion (quoted in Robert McFarlane's *The Old Ways*) that paths are imprinted with 'the dreams' of each traveller who had walked them and that 'walking up' by subsequent travellers would disturb what lay hidden, 'to flush out what is concealed' and recover what had gone before.[58]

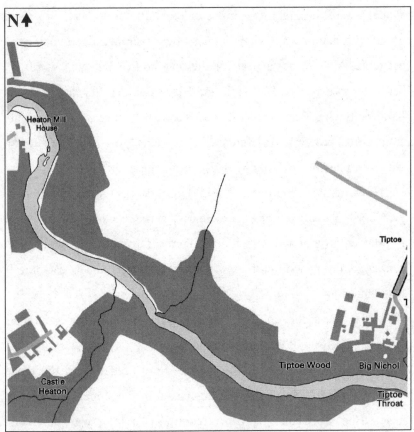

R. Till between Tiptoe Throat and Heaton Mill. Distance across the map from west to east is about half a mile. Contains Ordnance Survey data © Crown copyright and database right 2014.

Not a great deal is left of Castle Heaton and what there is, forms part of the present farm buildings. The castle remains are on private property and there is no public access. There are two buttresses set into the north-east wall of the stable, the probable remains of a turret and a rampart and a high, round tunnel vault within. Nevertheless, despite their paucity, the castle remains are listed as Grade II*.[59] Hutchinson, writing in 1776, says of Heaton:

an estate of the family of Greys, who were Governors of Norham, Wark, and Roxburgh, now in the possession of Lord Tankerville. The castle was of a square figure, and very strong; on the west side it had an area or court, called the Lion's Court; it sustained a siege by the Scots, before the battle of Flodden Field: on the north side was a vault capable of receiving an hundred horses or other cattle.[60]

John Leland, writing between 1535 and 1543, listed:

Eyton Castle longing to Ser Edward Graye. 2 Miles lower on Tyle then Etal. It stondithe on the west syd of Tylle. The Scotts at Floden Fild bet it sore.[61]

John Wallis, writing in 1769, says that:

in digging for stones [at Heaton Castle], two wells were discovered by the workmen, in which were found four pewter plates, with the arms of the *Greys* engraved upon them; also one bow made of *yew*. They came into the possession of Mr. *Gregson*, of *Wark* upon *Tweed*.[62]

Eneas Mackenzie, in 1825, mentions that:

A sword was found here a few years ago that probably belonged to some superior personage, from the hilt being wrapped with gold twist, and a small shield of silver inlaid on each side of the blade, with a cross thereon.[63]

He also says that in the time of Elizabeth I, the castle was described as 'a pleasaunt and beautifull beuilding in mannor square, with goodlie toweres and turrets'. In 1825, Heaton consisted of only one farmhold and a few cottages, much as it does today. Mawer gives the derivation of Heaton quite simply as, 'high farm'.[64]

Heaton is quite high above the R. Till because of the river gorge. It is part of the Castle Heaton and Shellacres Estate that straddles both sides of the R. Till and extends to about 1,229 acres. This is a good, agricultural and sporting estate comprising a country house at Castle Heaton, two arable farms with steadings and twelve cottages. A little to the north and down at river level is the site of Heaton Mill. This is where one of the Environment Agency's River Levels Stations is located (see pp. 5-6). It measures river levels and rates of flow at regular intervals, using an ultrasonic gauge measuring the full range of flows. The highest river level ever recorded here was 4.28 m.; this level was matched, exactly, during the wet winter of 2013/14. The gauges can just be seen in the photograph on p. 212.

Some traces of Heaton Mill remain. It is said that there is documentary evidence that a corn mill has been here since the 15th century and that the most recent mill buildings stood five storeys high before being demolished in 1953.[65] Demolition must have taken place long after the mill closed down because maps of the early 1920s show it as a disused mill. The height of the old mill building is borne out by the surviving walls and there is still evidence of the mill workings such as wheel-pits, the infilled mill-race and the controlling sluices and overflows. The weir upstream was set at an acute angle in the river in order to divert sufficient water to the mill. The miller's house and other buildings also survive as a private house; there is no public access to the old mill or any part of the buildings or to the river bank associated with it. Here, the river flows below sheer sandstone cliffs.

The *Berwickshire Advertiser* of 20th February 1841 reported a narrow escape by the miller, Mr. P. Nevins, who slipped off a plank across the mill-feed in trying to reach the sluice so as to turn it off. He fell into the wheel-pit and was caught by the revolving wheel but, fortunately, the revolution of the wheel carried him back up to the place where he had fallen and he was able to escape.[66]

Surviving walls from the old Heaton Mill giving some idea of its height. Photographs on this and the following page, taken by permission.

Until well into the 20th century, there was a historic ford next to the site of the old mill. This must have been used for many centuries, probably since, or even before, the time when the mill was first in existence. It is one of the supposed crossing points for the English army on the way to the Battle of Flodden. If the vanguard crossed lower down the river at Twizel, it is thought that the Earl of Surrey's forces may have crossed at Heaton. In the 1920s and 1930s, there were also stepping stones to assist pedestrian passage.

1. The infilled tail-race and cliffs at Heaton, top. 2. River level station, below.

212

Downstream from Heaton Mill, the R. Till takes some sharp turns as it passes Twizel Mill and flows on to Twizel Bridge, passing the Tillmouth Park Hotel and grounds on the west bank.

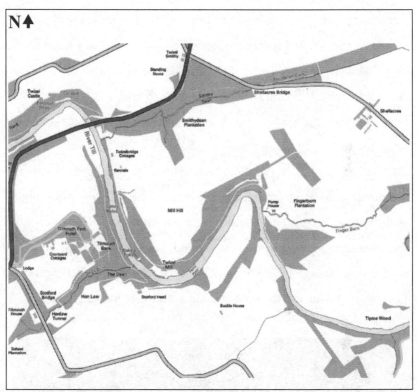

From Heaton and Tiptoe Wood to Twizel Bridge and beyond. Distance across map from west to east, about 1 mile. Contains Ordnance Survey data © Crown copyright and database right 2014.

There are a number of plants in the Tiptoe and Twizel area which, although not rare in the United Kingdom, are considered to be scarce or rare in north Northumberland and are recorded on the *Scarce, Rare & Extinct Vascular Plant Register* for north Northumberland, 2011.[67] These include Slender Tufted Sedge, *Carex acuta*; Dense Flowered Fumitory, *Fumaria densiflora*; Northern

213

Bedstraw, *Galium boreale*; Great Lettuce, *Lactuca virosa*; Cut Leaved Dead Nettle, *Lamium hybridum*; Toothwort, *Lathrea squamaria* and Common Fleabane, *Pulicaria dysenterica*. The last one had some medicinal use in the past for the treatment of dysentery but was probably used more often as an incense to drive away insects.

There are the remains of another ancient mill at Twizel on the north bank of the river, the site of which seems to have first been recorded in the 12th century.[68] The miller's house, a cottage that may have once been a stable and hayloft and outbuildings are still occupied but the two upper storeys and the roof of the mill have been demolished leaving the two intake arches at the lower level and surrounding walls at ground floor level. The drying kiln still remains with its roof. The grain would have been dried on the top floor and then fed through hoppers to the ground floor. Twizel Mill had two, low, breast wheels (where the water hit the wheels at axle height), the upper one of iron and the lower one of wood with an iron hub.

The remains of Twizel Mill with the upper storeys removed. The old high kiln is still standing. The weir to the left used to direct water to the two waterwheels.

214

Originally, the mill seems to have had an older part and was extended at a later date, when the weir may have been changed from a horseshoe shape to an oblique shape, which directed the water towards the twin arches and wheels. Today, the remains of the mill, the kiln, miller's house, cottages and farm buildings are in one, private, residential occupation and there is no public admittance to the old mill. When I was there, the river was full and the oblique weir was causing a contrast between the smooth surface of the water upstream and the turbulent flow of the river downstream.

Further downstream on the riverbank is a structure called Blake's Folly, incorporating a well-constructed, masonry arch. In 1810, Sir Francis Blake (1738-1818), 2nd Baronet, the owner of Tillmouth Park, situated on the west bank of the Till, had intended to build a bridge over the river as part of his improvements to the grounds but the bridge did not progress beyond the construction of the east pier with its overflow arch.[69]

Blake's Folly on the east bank, between Twizel Mill & Twizel Bridge.

Opposite Blake's Folly, on the west bank of the R. Till, Tillmouth Park and Garden with its country house (now The Tillmouth Park Hotel), extends from a point opposite Twizel Mill up to and beyond the A698 road, to include the ruined Twizel Castle. The land also extends westwards on both sides of the river as far as the railway viaduct and then on the north side of the river to Tillmouth and along the east bank of the R. Tweed as far as Twizel Boathouse. Alan Mawer tells us that 'Twizel' derives from OE *twislan*, meaning 'at the fork or junction of two streams'.[70]

Twizel Bridge at Grid Ref. NT88484330 is a medieval single-span bridge of early 16th century date, spanning the R. Till upstream from Twizel Castle. It is said to have been the widest single-span bridge in Britain until the 18th century. Vehicles crossed it until 1983 when a modern bridge was built to the south at Grid Ref. NT88504328. The bridge is listed Grade I, has a span of 27.5 m. and is built of squared stone with a single, segmental arch carried on five ribs. The plain parapets are carried on a series of corbels with a raised panel at the centre of the northern parapet and have been repaired and rebuilt in the 19th century.[71] During the 1980s the southern parapet at the west end was continued across the bridge to stop traffic. The length of the bridge, including abutments, is about 85 m. and it is 4 m. wide between parapets. Both abutments are wider than the bridge and are supported by buttresses; the angled, wing walls at the north-east end suggest that the road may have been realigned, long ago.

The bridge is said to have been built by the Selby family, possibly John Selby of Grindonrig who occupied Twizel Castle before the castle was bought by a kinsman, William Selby, in about 1520.[72]

The 16th century Twizel Bridge viewed from the modern road bridge.

The bridge is believed to have been built in 1511, two years before the Battle of Flodden in 1513 and it is accepted that some of the vanguard (probably guns and heavy equipment) of the English army under the command of the Earl of Surrey's eldest son, the Lord Admiral, Thomas Howard, crossed Twizel Bridge on its way to the battlefield.

Between about 1770 and 1820, Sir Francis Blake, when carrying out alterations at Twizel Castle, also did some alterations to the bridge. Extensive repairs and re-facing of stonework took place from the 18th century onwards. Structural repairs were carried out in 1977, to strengthen the bridge. An unusual, pre-fabricated pillbox was built close to the old bridge during the Second World War. The

217

modern, road bridge is built alongside the old bridge on its upstream side and is of functional, concrete construction. Leyland, in 1535-43, said that the old bridge was 'of one bow, but greate and stronge'.[73]

The modern, Twizel road bridge looking south from the old bridge.

To the north of the old Twizel Bridge and high above the cliff on the north bank of the R. Till (the cliff is shown on p. vi) is the Grade II* listed Twizel Castle.[74] Eneas Mackenzie tells us that the Twizel property was, in 1272, held in soccage tenure (a feudal tenure of land in return for agricultural or other non-military services such as the payment of rent) of the Mitford barons by Alicia de Merely and that, in 1329, it belonged, with Duddo, Grindon and most of the manor of Tillmouth, to Sir William Riddell. Sir William died without male issue and the manor became the property of the Herons before occupation passed by lease from William Heron to William Selby and then by outright ownership to another William Selby in 1525 (see p.

218

216).[75] It was during the time of the Herons that the castle was sacked in 1496 by James IV during his support for the pretender to the English throne, Perkin Warbeck.

The castle passed down to the Carrs of Ford Castle and, on the marriage of Elizabeth Carr, to Sir Francis Blake (1638-1718). As he had no son, it passed to his grandson, Sir Francis Blake (1708-1780), the 1st Baronet, who was a mathematician and supporter of the Whig government during the 1745 Jacobite rebellion. He died at Tillmouth, so there must have been a house there at that time. It was the 2nd Baronet, Sir Francis Blake (1738-1818) who commissioned James Nisbet of Kelso to incorporate the medieval ruin into a gothic house. The building works continued for about 50 years, starting in about 1770, but they never reached completion.[76]

The ruins of Twizel Castle, viewed from the north-east.

Today, the castle comprises a roofless, rectangular building of ashlar and squared stone, standing to a height of two storeys with wings on the north side and circular towers at each corner. There are four vaulted rooms along the south side, of ashlar construction; the vaults, the stone and brickwork were designed to minimize the risk of fire. The wings and the towers are the parts that Nisbet constructed and the medieval core has 1.5 m. thick walls. To the north of the building are lumps and bumps in the ground that are the remains of a garden and also some house platforms from a medieval village.

The castle may be approached from the minor road to the north, by a public footpath across the field in front of the castle but I prefer the approach from the small car park next to Twizel Bridge and up the footpath that climbs above the river. The castle is privately owned and is fenced off because of this but also because of its possibly dangerous condition. However, the public footpath passes right in front of the castle, giving a good view without having to enter the ruins. The castle is often described as an 18th century folly with a medieval core, but I think that 'folly' is a rather unfair description. Although the alterations and additions took a very long time and were never completed, they were not intended as a folly in the architectural sense even if it were a folly to attempt to construct such a massive building, the drawings of which show that it would have been a very stark building.

The castle stands above the sandstone cliffs of the river facing the grounds and gardens of Tillmouth Park House. The approach to the house is between a pair of gate lodges on the A698 road with the left-hand fork of the drive leading to the house entrance and the right-hand fork leading past a carriage house, dovecot, estate cottages and walled garden to the west frontage of the house. The original house was built in 1810 when Sir Francis Blake, the 2nd Baronet (who was a political writer) must have felt the need to establish himself somewhere other than in the ruins of Twizel Castle.

Tillmouth Park House (now Tillmouth Park Hotel), west frontage.

Sir Francis Blake (c. 1775-1860), 3rd Baronet, was MP for Berwick for many years until his defeat in 1835; he had no legitimate heir and the baronetcy became extinct. His illegitimate son, Francis Blake (1835-1909), suffered from heatstroke when serving as an army officer and entered a mental asylum in 1873, whilst retaining a life interest in the estate at Seghill. There is evidence in the Blake family papers of attempts to keep this episode within the family. After the death of the 3rd Baronet, the principal beneficiary apart from a bequest to his sister-in-law, Helen Blake, was Captain Francis Blake (1832-1861), whose son, Francis Douglas Blake (1856-1940) was created 1st Baronet in his own right in 1907. He was succeeded by his son, Sir Francis Edward Colquoun Blake (1893-1950), who was succeeded in turn by his son, Sir Francis Michael Blake (b. 1943), 3rd Baronet.

The house was rebuilt in the1870s and completed in 1882 by Sir Francis Blake, 1st Baronet, to designs by Charles Barry, junior, who recommended that Twizel Castle should be demolished, saying that he thought that he had never seen such an 'ill-adapted and ugly building' and that it 'impaired the beauty of its surroundings'. The castle was partly demolished and the stonework either sold or re-used in the reconstruction of Tillmouth Park House. One of the towers was gifted or sold to Horace St. Paul for re-erection at Ewart Park. The present Tillmouth House Hotel is an Elizabethan or Tudor style building of three storeys, built of ashlar stonework with a roof of Lakeland slate. The Elizabethan and Tudor styles are confirmed in the mullioned windows and the Tudor flowers on the parapet cornice. There is a very grand interior, incorporating features that were in the original house of 1810.

The grounds are extensive and include lawn, woodland, walled garden with alcove, formal gardens, kitchen gardens, riverside walk and two parkland/pleasure grounds, one of these leading down to the Dean Burn, a tributary of the Till which flows into the river on the west side, north-west of Twizel Mill.[77]

The Berwick Record Office, on behalf of The National Archives, holds the records of the Blake family of Ford, Twizel,

Tillmouth and Seghill (near Seaton Delaval, north of Newcastle), deposited there in 1990 by Sir Michael Blake.[78] The many documents cover the 16th to the 20th centuries and provide an in-depth record of property transactions, letters and other papers during that time. One of the earliest conveyances, in 1577, deals with the sale of the 'Manor and town of Twizel and pertinents' by William Carr to John Selby of Berwick-upon-Tweed for £600.[79]

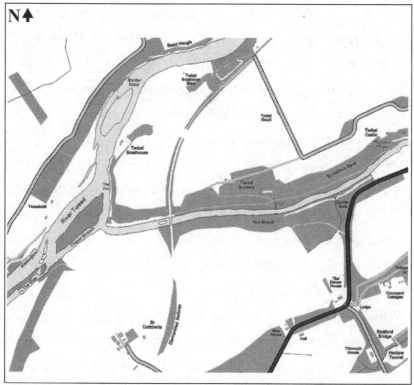

The final stretch of the R. Till from Twizel Castle to its confluence with the R. Tweed at Tillmouth. Distance across map from west to east is just over 1 mile. Contains Ordnance Survey data © Crown copyright and database right 2014.

From Twizel Bridge, the R. Till flows north-west and then south of west between the intriguingly named Penolive Wheel and St.

Helen's Bank on the north side and the equally intriguing Gutter Nick and Nut Wood on the south bank. These areas, on both banks, are within the Tillmouth Park property as far as the disused railway viaduct; thereafter this only includes the narrow, wooded strip on the north bank, as shown on the map. The OS maps show that the caption for the area marked 'Penolive Wheel' has moved from north-east of Twizel Bridge in the 1850s to below Twizel Castle, after 1959. Also after 1959, Bridgend Well disappears from the map, it having previously been shown to the east of the original Penolive Wheel.

Two other wells survive in this immediate area, Cat Well, just below Twizel Castle and St. Helen's Well, set within St. Helen's Bank. The first may well have been a source of water for the castle or for its outbuildings but St. Helen's Well is much lower down, accessed from the path along the north bank of the river. John Wallis, writing in 1769, describes:

> An upright rock, of a great size, and tapering to the top, about twenty feet high, a little below the bridge, on the edge of the *Till*; a fountain near it, consecrated to St. *Helen*, and by it an ancient sepulcure, said to have belonged to the family chapel.[80]

Wallis also describes at the same time, 'a sloping bank of hawthorn, in blossom beautiful' to the north of the bridge and 'the north-west side of the bridge adorned with large quantities of *Pellitory* of the *Wall*'. Pellitory-of-the-Wall, *Parietaria officinalis* or perhaps *Parietaria judaica*, is lichwort, a member of the nettle family but without stinging leaves. Both species have been the subject of discussion in the past as to their categorization.[81] They are quite inconspicuous plants with small, green or white flowers and are commonly found growing in crannies on dry walls and ruins, so well suited to the sandstone, Twizel cliffs. Lichwort has medicinal properties when made into an infusion, sometimes combined with wild carrot and parsley piert. If John Gerard(e) is to be believed, it seems to have had wondrous medicinal uses, being useful for urinary complaints, for coughs, for all kinds of skin complaints from spots to shingles to sunburn, for ear troubles and, as an ointment, for piles and gout, amongst many other things.[82]

St. Helen's Well and the 'deep defile' of Twizel's 'dim-wood glen' had significance for Sir Walter Scott in *Marmion*. The English army having crossed Twizel Bridge 'Where flows the sullen Till', Scott recounts how:

> Twisel! Thy rock's deep echo rang;
>
> And many a chief of birth and rank,
>
> Saint Helen! At thy fountain drank.
>
> Thy hawthorn glade, which now we see
>
> In spring-tide bloom so lavishly,
>
> Had them from many an axe its doom
>
> To give the marching columns room.[83]

St. Helen's Well, Twizel, is one of many holy wells in Britain dedicated to St. Helen or St. Helena (c. 248-c. 328), the mother of Constantine the Great and the patron saint of archaeology. St. Helen was converted to Christianity late in life and when Constantine gained the throne of the Western Roman Empire in 306, he treated her as royalty, enabling her to use her position to establish Christian churches throughout the empire. She led a group to the Holy Land to

225

search for the True Cross and excavated a site near Calvary where she discovered three crosses. She was recommended to take them to a woman who was near to death from an incurable disease; the woman touched them all and pronounced one of them to be the True Cross and, by doing so, was returned to health. St. Helen built a church on the spot and sent pieces of the cross to Rome and Constantinople. She also excavated nails and a piece of rope used to bind Jesus to the cross.

Geoffrey of Monmouth claimed that St. Helena was born in Britain, the daughter of Coel, Duke of Colchester, but there is no evidence for this (she was probably born somewhere in Asia Minor) and the legend may have arisen because Constantine had seen service in Britain with his father, Constantius, who was a Roman army officer. Also, there may have been confusion with the Welsh princess, St. Helen (or St. Elen of Carnafon), who founded churches in Wales during the 4th century.[84]

Downriver of St. Helen's Well, the R. Till flows beneath the impressive St. Cuthbert's Viaduct. The viaduct was built between 1846 and 1849 by the York, Newcastle & Berwick Railway and is a Grade II listed structure consisting of six, flat arches of rock-faced stone and brick, extending for 136 yards between abutments, with a height of 90 feet.[85] The branch line railway from Tweedmouth (Berwick) to Kelso via stations at Velvet Hall, Norham, Twizel, Coldstream, Sunilaws, Carham and Srouston, was operated by the North Eastern Railway as a result of a merger between the York, Newcastle & Berwick Railway and other companies. Twizel Station was situated to the north of the viaduct. The first train crossed the viaduct in July 1849 and the last goods train crossed in March 1965, the passenger service having ceased in June 1964. The viaduct is still in use as a public footpath and is maintained by the Highways Agency Historical Railways Estate.

St. Cuthbert's Viaduct, viewed from the west. Grid Ref. NT87314303.

The viaduct provides a lofty platform for views upstream and also downstream for looking along the final reach of the R. Till. Below the viaduct, I startled a pair of roe deer, *Capreolus capreolus*, that had come down to the riverbank to drink. They had their grey, winter coats; in summer, they would have had reddish brown coats and, if they were fauns, they would also have had attractive, white spots. They did not linger, but rushed off into the mixed vegetation that was gold, amber, burnt sienna and brown, in the low, winter sun.

227

R. Till looking west from St. Cuthbert's Viaduct towards the R. Tweed.

Downstream from the viaduct, the north bank is the wooded strip within the Tillmouth Park property. On the the south bank, a very narrow strip of willow and low-growing vegetation separates the river from a large, arable field belonging to St. Cuthbert's Farm. In 1825, Eneas Mackenzie wrote:

> Tillmouth chapel, dedicated to St. Cuthbert, and situated on a peninsula at the confluence of the Till and Tweed, is now in ruins. Not far from this ruined building, Sir Francis Blake, a few years ago, built a small chapel'.[86]

St. Cuthbert's chapel is still there in a ruined state (not on the map on p. 223—only the farm) and, in summer, is surrounded by crops. There is no sign of the other, small chapel. There is no evidence, either, of the medieval village of Tillmouth that was situated in this field but which is now only traceable from the air, by cropmarks.

228

St. Cuthbert's Chapel, Tillmouth. Seen in the distance in photo on p. 228.

The present chapel is said to date from the late 18th century or early 19th century and is built of dressed stone with a chamfered plint. It is built in the Gothic style and is on the site of an earlier chapel, first mentioned in 1311, of which nothing remains.[87] When the Berwickshire Naturalists' Club visited 'Tillmouth Chapel' in May 1909, it was said that the ancient chapel was dedicated to St. Catherine and that it had been a gift of the lords of Tillmouth and endowed with a carucate of land (equal to the area that could be ploughed by one team of oxen in a year, perhaps 120 acres) from their estate.

It was also said that, by an Inquisition in 1311, with local vicars as jurors, it seemed that the chapel had been vacant since the feast of the Ascension following the death of John de Molveston. Sir

229

William Rydel (sic) was the patron and he had presented John de Kelsey, presumably as the chaplain. Nicholas de Lesseberry was ordained Deacon at Auckland in 1337, on the strength of the title of the chantry of the chapel of St. Catherine of 'Tyllemuth', given to him by Walter Crayk. In the 18th century, the altar window was in place (as it is today, although with a settlement fracture below), there was a basin set into the south wall and the foundations of the minister's house were also visible on the north side.[88]

St. Catherine of Alexandria was a young woman of noble birth who, in the 4th century, enraged the Emperor Maximilian by trying to persuade him not to worship false gods. She out-debated the greatest scholars and philosophers set against her by the Emperor and converted them, as well as the Empress, to Christianity. Catherine was condemned to torture on the wheel but it shattered when she touched it. She was beheaded and the angels carried her body to Mt. Sinai where, later, a church and a monastery were built in her name. St. Catherine is the patron saint of unmarried women, students, craftsmen who use a wheel, lacemakers and milliners.

In the medieval village of Tillmouth, there was a tower that was destroyed by James IV in 1496; English Heritage gives the date of its construction as 1415 onwards.[89] In 1551, the inspection of the frontiers and marches between England and Scotland by Sir Robert Bowes and Sir Raufe Elleker, describes the medieval village of 'Tilmouthe' as:

> Fyrste upon the ryv' of Twede & upon the west side of the
> ryv' of Tyll nere unto where the same ryvr' fallethe into
> Twede standeth a towne called Tylmouthe of the

inherytaunce of one...Claveringe being at this p^esent a childe wth in age. In the same towne be tenne husbandlands well plenyshed and in yt standeth a pece of an olde tower which was casten downe brenghte & defaced by a knyghte of Scottes in a warre tyme more than fortye yeres paste. And yet standeth more the half p'te of the vawtes & walls of the same tower. The costes of the repayringe whereof ys esteemed to amount & extende nere unto one hundredth m'ks.[90]

Eneas Mackenzie mentions that:

Near this place lay till recently the remains of a stone boat or coffin, in which, tradition says, the body of St. Cuthbert was miraculously conveyed down the Tweed from Melros [sic].

"In his stone coffin down he rides,

(A pond'rous bark for river tides)

Yet light as gossamer it glides

Downwards to Tillmouth's cell"

Marmion, canto 2.[91]

Mackenzie also quotes from Gough's additions to Camden's *Britannica*, when he said that 'it is a stone boat, of as fine a shape as a boat of wood'. It was described as being:

nine feet three inches in length—its mean outside breadth, three feet three inches—the height, one foot nine inches—and the thickness, four and a half inches...it would displace $3287^1/_2$ lb. of water, and would weigh 3125 lb. The difference, $162^1/_2$ lb. is the additional weight the boat would carry, which is equal to that of a man near twelve stone in weight.

In 1776, Hutchinson wrote that:

> It is said that not long ago there was a design to convert this hallowed vessel to mean offices, a peasant having devised to pickle pork in it, or thereout to feed his hogs: to preserve it from such profanation, the spirits of darkness brake it in the night, leaving the fragments near the chapel.[92]

Despite the spirits leaving the fragments near the chapel, they are no longer there and their whereabouts are unknown. OS maps from the mid 19th century onwards show the site of another holy well, St. Cuthbert's Well, to the east of the ruined chapel.

St. Cuthbert was born in 635 in the vicinity of Melrose and spent his early years as a soldier in the army of Northumbria before entering the monastery at Melrose and then becoming master at Ripon. He became Prior of Melrose in 664 after the death of Boisil but was almost immediately sent to Lindisfarne where he was instumental in implementing the transition to Roman Christianity from the Celtic tradition, as decreed by the Synod of Whitby. Bede gives a detailed account of Cuthbert's life on Lindisfarne including his time as a hermit on St. Cuthbert's Island and on the Farne Islands (where eider ducks are still known as 'Cuddy's ducks') and his final appointment as Bishop of Lindisfarne before his death in 687.[93]

After his death, Cuthbert was credited with miraculous powers in healing the sick and one of the main reasons for his veneration must have been that when, eleven years after his death, the monks reburied his body in a new coffin in a tomb above the floor, they found that his body was 'intact and whole as if it were alive, the joints of the limbs flexible and much more like a sleeping than a dead

232

man'.[94] Bede died in 735 before the first of the Viking raids and his history does not therefore describe how Cuthbert's body was removed from Lindisfarne and carried around the Northumberland countryside for seven years in order to prevent its capture, before being kept temporarily in Chester-le-Street, Ripon and Durham. Perhaps the stone coffin-boat at Tillmouth was associated with this seven-year period of 'wandering' but it seems rather unlikely as there would have been less difficult ways to transport the body in secrecy. When St. Cuthbert was finally reburied in Durham Cathedral in 1104, his body was still in a state of perfect preservation.

The end of the journey. The R. Tweed looking upriver at the Chapel Stream branch of the river that flows around one side of an island. The R. Till is seen flowing into the Tweed from the left hand side.

Beyond the viaduct, I walked down the path on the north bank opposite St. Cuthbert's Chapel to reach the confluence of the R. Till and the R. Tweed at Chapel Stream and I sat on a convenient bench to take stock. It was a sunny, winter's day, reasonably mild and the waters of both rivers were as smooth as glass. I felt a sense of regret that I had come to the end of my journey but I felt grateful for having experienced so many interesting things on the way. The first thought that struck me was the contrast between the wildness of Breamish Head and the serenity of Chapel Stream at Tillmouth and I then reflected on the variety of the landscapes that I had seen in between those two places.

I had travelled down the two rivers in spring, summer, autumn and winter. Now, at Chapel Stream, the vegetation was in winter clothing so I could only imagine what it was like when the Berwickshire Naturalists' Club was here in 1909, looking at the 'strip of Beech that fringed its banks' and which 'attracted the eye by its rich vernal beauty', the 'fragrant Gorse and bursting Lilac', the 'profusion of Primroses that enlivened the shade' and the 'Meadow Saxifrage and Mountain Speedwell' that 'lent variety to the fresh verdure that clothed both banks to the water's edge'.[95] I determined to come back here in the spring but, just now, the winter landscape had a look and an atmosphere all of its own and I felt that it was just as special in its own way.

I had come across so much history and archaeology along the way, all of it interesting. The profusion of hillforts, rock-art and ancient settlement sites confirmed the intense level of human activity in Northumbria in prehistoric times. The number, scale and siting of castles confirmed what a dangerous area this was during the constant raids, battles and skirmishes raging across the Border country during the medieval period. The large number of peles, bastles and tower

234

houses confirmed that the threat from marauders was at such a level that even domestic dwellings and farmsteads had to be built so that they could withstand attack and siege.

Whilst sitting on the bench, I had a feeling of optimism about the future of the R. Breamish and the R. Till and it wasn't just because the sun was shining. From what I had seen along the way and discovered in my researches, it seemed that there was a determination by the many public and private organizations and individuals that the two rivers should be well looked after and managed for their own benefit, for the benefit of the people who live nearby and for the benefit of visitors to the area. River conservation and management has improved a great deal in recent years, helped by scientific research and by changes in attitude. This has been reflected in legislation on a whole range of matters to do with the environment, wildlife and in new techniques for helping the rivers when they are under stress due to threats such as climate change, flooding, pollution and erosion.

Earlier, I touched on the work carried out by the Environment Agency in relation to such matters as water abstraction, water sampling and flood control and relief where safeguards have become more stringent in recent years. I have mentioned other public bodies such as the Northumberland National Park Authority, Northumberland County Council, the Forestry Commission, the Tweed Commission, the Tweed Forum, Natural England, English Heritage and Northumberland Wildlife Trust, all of them involved in the care of and improvement of the rivers and their catchment areas for a whole range of reasons. Five years ago, the Environment Agency established a forward-thinking partnership entitled 'Cheviot

Futures' identifying the challenges to be faced by communities as a result of climate change and providing solutions to those challenges. This is a partnership of cross-border agencies, including those mentioned above as well as others others and includes not just the Cheviot Hills, but also the northern river catchments (Breamish, Till, Glen, Bowmont, Wooler Water and Teviot). The project is undertaking a wide range of studies and carrying out practical projects arising from those studies.[96]

I have also been struck by the beneficial work being carried out by private estates and individuals, such as woodland or other environmental improvements. Private companies involved in commercial activities such as sand and gravel extraction have restored disused workings (as a result of planning conditions) and have produced first class nature and wildlife habitats that can also help with drainage and potential flooding problems.

On a final note, it has been encouraging to see commercial enterprises co-operating so well with the archaeology world by allowing excavations to take place on land where extraction is taking place. In this regard, I am thinking particularly of the Milfield Plain.

~

So that brings me to the end of my long and very interesting journey. I have enjoyed it so much that I would like to start it all over again—perhaps I will.

Notes

CHAPTER 1—Setting the Scene

1. Natural England, Environment Agency, Tweed Forum, *River Till Restoration Strategy*, March 2013, p.11

2. *The Till and Breamish Catchment Flood Management Plan*, Environment Agency, Leeds, 2009

3. Oughton, Dr. Elizabeth; Passmore, Dr. David; Dilley, Mr. Luke, *Cheviots Flood Impact Study*, Centre for Rural Economy, Newcastle University, 2009

4. The three stations can be accessed online at www.environment-agency.gov.uk/homeandleisure/floods/riverlevels/120580.aspx?RegionId=3&AreaId=8&CatchmentId=31

5. *Minerals and Waste Monitoring Report 2009/2010 Low Hedgeley Quarry*, Inspection 12 November 2009, Northumberland County Council

6. Lawrence, D.J.D.; Arkley, S.L.B.; Everest, J.D.; Clarke S.M.; Millward D.; Hyslop, E.K.; Thompson, G.L.; Young, B., *Northumberland National Park Geodiversity Audit and Action Plan*, British Geolog. Survey, Nottingham, 2007, p 18

7. ibid. Information sourced from diagram on p. 19

8. ibid., p. 23

9. ibid., pp. 56-7

10. ibid., pp. 60-3

11. ibid., pp. 64-5

12. *Water abstraction getting the balance right The Till Catchment Abstraction Management Strategy*, Environment Agency, Bristol, 2008

13. *Till and Northumberland Rivers Groundwater Quality Review*, prepared by Environmental Simulations International Limited for the Environment Agency, September 2008

14. See: www.northumberlandnationalpark.org.uk/understanding/wildlifehabitats/riversburns

15. Two reports that give credence to this view are, firstly, *Mapping Tranquility* commissioned by the Campaign to Protect Rural England (CPRE) and the Countryside Agency. The report was carried out by The Centre for Environmental and Spatial Analysis and Participatory Evaluation and Appraisal in Newcastle upon Tyne (PEA NuT) both at Northumbria University and The Landscape Research

Group, University of Newcastle, 2005. Secondly, see *Developing an Intrusion Map of England* prepared for CPRE by Land Use Consultants, London, 2007

16. There is a great deal of information on the Environment Agency's website at www.environment-agency.gov.uk from where various links are possible to specific information and maps

17. Mackenzie, Eneas, *An Historical, Topographical and Descriptive View of the County of Northumberland and of those Parts of the County of Durham situated north of the River Tyne...*, Volume II, Second Edition, 1825, p. 15. Maclauclan, Henry, *Memoir written during A Survey of the Eastern Branch of Watling Street...*, written for private distribution, London, 1864, p.22

~

CHAPTER 2—Breamish Head to Ingram Bridge

1. Mawer, Allen, *The Place-Names of Northumberland and Durham*, Cambridge at The University Press, 1920, p. 102. In the Borders, there is a mixture of Old English, Middle English, Modern English and Scots language derivatives and dialects in place-names as well as those of Celtic origin. In addition to Mawer's work, it is useful to consult Ordnance Survey guides to place names such as *Guide to Scots origins of place names in Britain*, 2004 and the *Glossary of Scots origins of place names in Britain*, although these may not be infallible because of the difficulties experienced by the surveyors in understanding explanations from local people

2. See ed. Hardy, Dr. James, *The Denham Tracts A Collection of Folklore...*,,etc., Vol. II, London, 1895, p. 120. Thomas Pringle, the poet, associated a 'mountain spirit' with the Hanging Stone; the stone is said to have acquired its name from when a packman was resting on it with his cloth-covered bundle too near the edge. The pack slipped over and its belt tightened around the packman's neck, strangling him. The same thing happened to a robber who was carrying off a stolen sheep. Both man and sheep were hanged

3. For more information on feral goats in Britain, see the information provided by the British Feral Goat Research Group on www.britishferalgoat.org.uk and information in different locations on the Northumberland National Park Authority website

4. Mackenzie, Eneas, Volume I, Second Edition, 1825, p. 171

5. For a comprehensive account of the beer and whisky trade in Upper Coquetdale, see *The Production and Trade of Beer and Whisky in Upper Coquetdale*, produced for Northumberland National Park Authority by The Archaeological Practice Ltd., 2006

6. The Otterburn Ranges Access Map and Guide; The Otterburn Ranges Open Access Area, both available from National Park Information Centres and other outlets.

7. For more information on National Parks, see www.nationalparks.gov.uk/home; for Northumberland National Park, visit www.northumberlandnationalpark.org.uk/

8. Mawer, Allen, pp. 25, 234

9. For detailed information on the Cheviot breed, see the website of the Cheviot Sheep Society, www.cheviotsheep.org

10. For detailed information on Blackface sheep and North of England Mules, see the

NOTES

website for the Blackface Sheep Breeders' Association, www.scottish-blackface.co.uk and the website for the North of England Mule Sheep Association, www.nemsa.co.uk/north-england-mule

11. Brown, Kit, *A Survey of the Extent and Condition of Ancient Woodlands in Northumberland*, Northumberland Native Woodland Project, 2006; *Native Woodland Habitat Action Plan* within the heading of Northumberland Biodiversity Action Plan, 2008; *Ancient and Semi-Natural Woodland Habitat Action Plan*, Northumberland National Park

12. For information on woodland proposals by the Linhope Estate, see the Minutes of the Northumberland National Park Authority of 15th September 2010, Item 7. Also, see maps prepared by the Authority showing (1) existing woodland on the Linhope Estate (Map Centre: 971148, 12 August 2010) and (2) proposed native woodland planting (Map Centre: NT960150).

13. See *Keys to the Past*, providing online access to archaeological and historic records of the counties of Northumberland and Durham; Durham County Council and Northumberland County Council www.keystothepast.info/Pages/home.aspx

14. Mackenzie, Eneas, Volume II, Second Edition, 1825, p. 21

15. Extract reproduced from *A Vision of Britain through Time*, University of Portsmouth and others, see www.visionofbritain.org.uk/place/21513

16. *Keys to the Past* record for Greaves Ash Camp, ref. N1254

17. Mawer, Allen, pp. 4, 236

18. *Keys to the Past* record for Hartside Hill, ref. N1291

19. Dickens, Tony, *The River Bridges of Northumberland, Vol. I, The River Till and its Tributaries*, 1975, p. 9

20. The Northumberland National Park Authority publishes excellent booklets and leaflets on the archaeology of the Breamish Valley. A handy free leaflet is *The Breamish Valley. Walk in a landscape of ancestors*. A useful booklet (not free) is *People of the Breamish Valley. Discovering our hillfort heritage*

21. Young, Dr. Robert; Frodsham, Paul; Hedley, Iain; Speak, Steven; *An Archaeological Framework for Northumberland National Park-Resource Assessment, Research Agenda and Research Strategy*. Available to download as a PDF document from www.northumberlandnationalpark.org

22. Alnham Village Atlas, compiled by The Archaeological Practice Ltd, commissioned by The Northumberland National Park Authority, p. 27. The references within the extract relate to Cowen, J D, Prehistoric section, in *A History of Northumberland. XIV: The Parishes of Alnham, Chatton, Chillingham, Eglingham, Ilderton, Ingram and Whittingham. The Chapelries of Lowick and Doddington*, (ed.) M. Hope Dodds, Newcastle upon Tyne, 1935, pp. 21-67; Higham, N, *The Northern Counties to AD 1000*, London, 1986

23. See The Northumberland National Park data sheet on Prehistoric Archaeology accessible online at www.northumberlandnationalpark.org.uk/__data/assets/pdf_file/0003/148503/arf-4.prehistory.pdf; the reference to the cauldron draws on Burgess, C., *Bronze Age*

Metalwork in Northern England c.1000 to 700BC, Oriel Press, Newcastle upon Tyne, 1968

24. *Historia de Sancto Cuthberto*, published in two editions: *Symeonis Dunelmensis Opera et Collectanea* (ed.) J Hodgson Hinde, Surtees Society **41**, I, 138-52 (Durham, 1868). *Symeonis Monachi Opera Omnia* (ed.) T. Arnold, Rolls Series **75**, I, 196-214 (London, 1882)

25. Mackenzie, Eneas, Volume II, Second Edition, 1825, p. 27

26. Reid, A, *A History of Northumberland*, Northumberland County History Committee, Vol. 14, 1935, pp. 457-81

27. Frodsham, P. and Waddington, C, *The Breamish Valley Archaeology Project*, 1994-2002, pub. 2004. In. P. Frodsham (ed.) *Archaeology in Northumberland National Park*. York, Council for British Archaeology: 171-189. See also, *Ingram Village Atlas*, The Archaeological Practice for The Northumberland National Park Authority, 2004, p. 33

CHAPTER 3—Ingram Bridge to Bewick Bridge

1. The Northumberland National Park website page: www.nnpa.org.uk/understanding/historyarchaeology/historicvillageatlas/ingramintroduction/ingramhistory/ingramwatermills

2. For a more detailed introduction to cultivation terraces and field systems, see *Introductions to Heritage Assets: Field Systems*, English Heritage

3. *Keys to the Past* record for Brandon Chapel, ref. N3094

4. Mackenzie, Eneas, Volume II, Second Edition, 1825, p. 18

5. Camden, William, *Britain, or a Chorographicall Description of the most flourishing Kingdomes, England, Scotland and Ireland* (London: George Bishop and John Norton, 1610) Copyright 2004 by Dana F. Sutton. This text was transcribed by Prof. Sutton of the University of California, Irvine from Philemon Holland's 1610 translation [British Library *Short Title Catalogue* 4509, *Early English Books* reel 911:1]. This extract quoted ftom A Vision of Britain Through Time: www.visionofbritain.org.uk/travellers/Camden/29#pn_92

6. Metherell, Chris, *Scarce, Rare & Extinct Vascular Plant Register*, North Northumberland Vice County 68, 2011

7. Wallis, John, *The Natural History and Antiquities of Northumberland...* Vol. II, printed for the author, London, 1769, p. 492

8. Dickens, Tony, p. 12

9. Source—Northumberland County Council

10. For information on this and other disused stations, see www.disused-stations.org.uk

11. For more information on Hedgeley, Low Hedgeley and Branton Quarries restoration programmes, see the annual *Minerals and Waste Site Monitoring Reports* for each quarry downloadable from www.northumberland.gov.uk

NOTES

12. To see the reasons for notification as an SSSI and the list of aquatic plants, animals and insects contributing to that special status, see website showing the Notification to the Secretary of State on 1 November 1999 on www.english-nature.org.uk/citation/citation_photo/2000288.pdf

13. Natural England, Environment Agency, Tweed Forum, *River Till Restoration Strategy*, March 2013 available to view online at: http://tweedforum.org/projects/current-projects/TRRS_web.pdf

14. Mawer, Allen, pp. 109, 237

15. See British Listed Buildings website www.britishlistedbuildings.co.uk: Percy's Cross-English Heritage ID: 236558

16. Hall, Rev. G. Rome, 'Notes on Modern Survivals of Ancient Well-Worship in North Tynedale, in connection with the Well of Coventina at Carrawbrough (Procolitia), on the Roman Wall', *ARCHÆOLOGIA ÆLIANA...*, Society of Antiquaries of Newcastle, Volume VIII, Newcastle, 1880, p. 62. See also ed. Hardy, Dr. James, *The Denham Tracts,* Vol. II, pp. 151-157

17. Hope, Robert Charles, *The Legendary Lore of the Holy Wells of England...,* Elliot Stock, London, 1893, pp. 100-115

18. See British Listed Buildings website www.britishlistedbuildings.co.uk: Hedgeley Hall-English Heritage ID 236579; Crawley Tower-English Heritage ID 236575. For Crawley Tower earthworks, see the Ancient Monuments website: www.ancientmonuments.info/ennd64-earthwork-at-crawley-tower

19. Wilson, John Marius, *Imperial Gazetteer of England and Wales*,transcribed on the Vision of Britain website www.visionofbritain.org.uk/place/8717

20. Mackenzie, Eneas, Volume II, Second Edition, 1825, pp. 16-17

21. Hedley, Rev. Anthony, 'An Essay towards ascertaining the Etymology of the Names of Places in the County of Northumberland' *ARCHÆOLOGIA ÆLIANA...*, Society of Antiquaries of Newcastle, Volume I, Newcastle, 1822, p. 257

22. *Keys to the Past* record for The Ringses, ref. N3145

23. *Keys to the Past* record for Beanley Tile Works, ref. N14557

24. *The Scots Peerage*, ed. Sir James Balfour Paul, Lord Lyon King of Arms, Edinburgh, 1906, pp. 246-50

25. ibid.

26. Mackenzie, Eneas, Volume II, Second Edition, 1825, pp. 16/17

27. Hodgson, J. C., 'The Hospital of St. Lazarus and the Manor of Harehope', *ARCHÆOLOGIA ÆLIANA...*, Society of Antiquaries of Newcastle, Third Series Volume XIX, Newcastle, 1822, p. 76-82

28. Dickens, Tony, pp. 14-15

29. Hodgson, J. C., pp. 76-82

30. Dickens, Tony, pp. 14-15

31. *Keys to the Past* record for Old Bewick Camp, ref. N3605

32 Mackenzie, Eneas, Volume II, Second Edition, 1825, p. 15

33. ibid.

34. *Keys to the Past* record for Bewick, ref. N12993

35. Education Enquiry. *Abstract of the Answers and Returns made pursuant to An Address of the House of Commons dated 24th May 1833*, Vol. II, Leicester—Suffolk, 20 March 1835, p. 690

36. *Keys to the Past* record for Stone Cross (Bewick), ref. N3617

CHAPTER 4—Bewick Bridge to Chatton Bridge

1. Oxford Dictionaries online: www.oxforddictionaries.com/definition/english/till-4 www.englandsnortheast.co.uk/PlaceNameMeaningsTtoY.html; Shaw, Rev. William, *Gallic and English Dictionary*, Volume I, London, 1780

2. Mackenzie, Eneas, Volume II, Second Edition, 1825, p. 15 He draws on the Rev. Anthony Hedley's essay in *ARCHÆOLOGIA ÆLIANA...*, Society of Antiquaries of Newcastle, Volume I, Newcastle, 1822, p. 257 and also draws on two other authorities, Jamieson and Bullet

3. Mackichan, Dr. N. D., 'Did a Shire of Whittingham ever exist?, *Records and Recollections*, The Aln and Breamish Local History Society, New Series Volume I, No. 4, June 2005, p. 5

4. Dickens, Tony, pp. 15-16

5. Mackenzie, Eneas, Volume II, Second Edition, 1825, p. 15

6. For more information see www.forestry.gov.uk/pdf/nee-eia-appendix-2-sssi.pdf/$file/nee-eia-appendix-2-sssi.pdf

7. For more detailed information, see British Geological Survey record at http://data.bgs.ac.uk/doc/Lexicon/NamedRockUnit/RDCO.html and also the Northumberland Nation Park website under: www.northumberlandnationalpark.org.uk/understanding/geology/geologicalhistory/carboniferousrocks/carboniferoussuccession

8. *Keys to the Past* ref. N3484

9. See the Pillbox Study Group website-Northumberland at: www.pillbox-study-group.org.uk/index.php/defence-articles/northumberland-stoplines/

10. Dickens, Tony, p. 18

11. Description from *The National Gazetteer of Great Britain and Ireland* (1868) Transcribed by Colin Hinson ©2003

12. Tate, George, *The History of the Borough, Castle, and Barony of Alnwick*, Vol. I, Henry Hunter Blair, Alnwick, 1876, p. 439

13. Bowes, Sir Robert; Ellerker, Sir Rauffe, Knights Commissioners, *A View and Survey of the East and Middle Marches of England*, 2 Dec. 1542, 33, H. s, Cotton MS. Caligula, B. 8. Reproduced in Hodgson, John, *A History of Northumberland in Three Parts*, Part III. Vol. II, Article III, p. 184

14 *Keys to the Past* refs. N2808, N3426 & N3603

15. Mackenzie, Sir James D., *The Castles of England Their Story and Structure*, Vol. II, The Macmillan Co., New York, 1896, p. 393

16. ibid.

17. Bowes, Sir Robert; Ellerker, Sir Rauffe, Knights Commissioners, Vol. II, Article III, p. 209

18. Bates, Cadwaller John, *The Border Holds of Northumberland*, Volume I, Andrew Reid, Sons & Co., London and Newcastle-Upon-Tyne, 1891, p. 302. Reproduced in *ARCHAEOLOGICA ÆLIANA...*, Volume XIV, Society of Antiquaries of Newcastle-Upon-Tyne, Andrew Reid, Sons & Co., London and Newcastle-Upon-Tyne, 1891

19. *Keys to the Past* ref. N3391

20. Mawer, Allen, p. 169

21. ibid, p. 45

22. Mackenzie, Eneas, Volume I, Second Edition, 1825, pp. 389-90

23. ibid.

24. Bowes, Sir Robert; Ellerker, Sir Rauffe, Knights Commissioners, Vol. II, Article III, p. 209

25. Donaldson, James, *Modern Agriculture or the Present State of Husbandry in Great Britain...*Vol. II, Edinburgh, 1796, pp. 67-70

26. *Keys to the Past* refs. N3393, N3394, N3427; Mackenzie, Eneas, Volume I, Second Edition, 1825, p. 391

27. Mackenzie, Eneas, Volume II, Second Edition, 1825, pp. 12-15

28. *Keys to the Past* ref. N3479

29. Survey of Astronomical History, Society for the History of Astronomy: see online at: http://shasurvey.wordpress.com/england/northumberland/

30. *Keys to the Past* ref. N20340

31. Family Search, Community Trees, Person ID 167481 http://histfam.familysearch.org/index.php

32. *Keys to the Past* ref. N22563

33. Dickens, Tony, p. 20

34. ibid.

35. English Heritage listing ID 237474

36. Dickens, Tony, p. 20

37. Mawer, Allen, p. 43

38. Mackenzie, Eneas, Volume I, Second Edition, 1825, pp. 386-7

39. ibid.

40. ibid.

41. William Whellan & Co., *History, Topography, and Directory of Northumberland...*, Whittaker and Co., London and Manchester, 1856, p. 677

42. ibid.

43. *Keys to the Past* ref. N3470

44. Tillside website-Chatton Ward: www.tillside.org.uk/Tillside_Chatton.htm

45. Kerridge, Eric, *Agrarian Problems in the Sixteenth Century and After*, Routledge, Abingdon, 1969, p. 128

46. *Keys to the Past* refs. N3430, N3431, N21785, N21800

47. Details from Durham Mining Museum: www.dmm.org.uk/colliery/c065.htm

~

CHAPTER 5—Chatton Bridge to Doddington Bridge

1. *Keys to the Past* refs. N3414, N3396, N13331

2. Dickens, Tony, p. 22

3. Mackenzie, Eneas, Volume I, Second Edition, 1825, p. 387

4. See V.A.D. Hospitals in Northumberland and Durham 1914-1918 www.donmouth.co.uk/local_history/VAD/VAD_hospitals.html

5. For information and listing of POW camps in England, see Thomas, Roger J.C., *Prisoner of War Camps (1939-1948), Twentieth Century Recording Project*, English Heritage, 2003

6. Dickens, Tony, p. 22

7. Mawer, Allen, p. 89

8. Mackenzie, Eneas, Volume I, Second Edition, 1825, p. 388

9. For a detailed account of the Culley Brothers and their achievements, see the excellent paper—*Matthew & George Culley*, The Glendale Gateway Trust, The Cheviot Centre, Wooler

10. Mackenzie, Eneas, Volume I, Second Edition, 1825, p. 388

11. *Keys to the Past* ref. N3810

12. ibid., refs. N3301, N3338

13. English Heritage listing ID 237502

14. Dickens, Tony, pp. 25-7

15. Mackenzie, Eneas, Volume I, Second Edition, 1825, p. 388

16. English Heritage listing ID 237503

17. *Keys to the Past* ref. N3298

18. See the Northumberland Rock Art website pages for Cuddy's Cave at http://rockart.ncl.ac.uk/panel_detail.asp?pi=97

19. Dickens, Tony, pp. 25-7, 31-2

NOTES

20. Mackenzie, Eneas, Volume I, Second Edition, 1825, p. 382

21. See Wooler and Glendale Community website: www.wooler.org.uk/places/410-doddington and Northumberland Communities website: http://communities.northumberland.gov.uk/Doddington.htm

22. English Heritage listing ID 237716

23. ibid., ID 237714

~

CHAPTER 6—Doddington Bridge to Ford Bridge

1. English Heritage listing ID 237721

2. Dickens, Tony, p. 33

3. Nennius, *History of the Britons (Historia Brittonum)*, transl. J. A. Giles from *Six Old English Chronicles*, ed. J. A. Giles, Henry G. Bohn, London, 1948, Ch. 50

4. Bede, *The Ecclesiastical History of the English People*, ed. Judith McLure & Roger Collins, Oxford University Press, Oxford World's Classics (paperback), 2008, pp. 97-8

5. Mawer, Allen, p. 79. This describes the enclosure between the Till and the Glen

6. Mackenzie, Eneas, Volume I, Second Edition, 1825, pp. 382-3

7. Parson, Wm. & White, Wm., *History, Directory and Gazetteer of the Counties of Durham and Northumberland*, Newcastle, 1828, pp. 503-4

8. ibid.; also Mackenzie, as above; also Lodge, Edmund, *The Peerage and Baronetage of the British Empire*, Hurst and Blackett, 1869, pp. 805-6

9. Mackenzie, Eneas, Volume I, Second Edition, 1825, p. 383

10. Portable Antiquities Scheme-Swords. See: http://finds.org.uk/bronzeage/objects/swords

11. *Keys to the Past* ref. N13256

12. Blockwell, Albert, *Diary of a Red Devil, By Glider to Arnhem with the 7th King's Own Scottish Borderers*, Helion & Company Limited, Solihull, 2005

13. *Keys to the Past* ref. N2160

14. Mawer, Allen, pp. 84-5

15. Mackenzie, Eneas, Volume I, Second Edition, 1825, p. 395

16. Charlton, John, Remembering Slavery   Slave trade, slavery and abolition: the north east of England connections, Archive Mapping and Research Project, led by the Literacy and Philosophical Society (Lit&Phil), Newcastle, 2007; North East Slavery & Abolition Group E Newsletter No. 9, September 2010

17. *Keys to the Past* refs. N2131, N2205, N2206, N20470

18. ibid., N1953, N19724

19. For information on the life of Josephine Butler, see information and letters held by The Women's Library, London Metropolitan University. Extracts from the letters

can be viewed online on the National Archives website at:
http://nationalarchives.gov.uk/A2A/records.aspx?cat=106-3jbl_2&cid=-1#-1

20. *New Sporting Magazine*, May 1834, p. 421

21. *Keys to the Past* ref. N2135

22. English Heritage Building ID: 237624

23. Erskine, John, *An Institute of the Law of Scotland in Four Books, A New Edition with Additional Notes by James Ivory in Two Volumes*, Edinburgh, 1824, pp. 437-447

24. Young, Dr. Robert; Frodsham; Paul, Hedley, Iain; Speak, Steven, *An Archaeological Research Framework for Northumberland National Park Resource Assessment, Research Agenda and Research Strategy*, undated but post 2004, pp. 203-5

25. Leaflet on RAF Milfield produced for the Maelmin Heritage Trail. See also: www.maelmin.org.uk

26. Articles in *The Northumberland Gazette*, *The Journal* and by the Mineral Products Association:
http://www.mineralproducts.org/awards11_woodbridge_quarry.htm

27. See Archaeology Data Service at:
http://archaeologydataservice.ac.uk/archives/view/cheviot_eh_2008

28. See the Maelmin Trail website: www.maelmin.org.uk

29. Bede, p. 98 (Bede II 14)

30. Fox, Bethany, *A Journal of Early Medieval Northwestern Europe*, Issue 10 (May 2007) 'Place-Names of North-East England and South-East Scotland', The Heroic Age

31. For much more information, see ARS Ltd Report No. 2007/14 March 2007 and ARS Report No, 2009/27 April 2009, both accessed through 'Downloads' from this page of the ARS website: www.archaeologicalresearchservices.com/projects/lanton-quarry

32. SINE website page:
http://sine.ncl.ac.uk/view_structure_information.asp?struct_id=995

33. Sykes, John, *Local Records or Historical Register of Remarkable Events*, printed in Newcastle, 1824, p. 271

34. Dickens, Tony, pp. 43, 52

35. ibid., p. 43

36. Natural England, Environment Agency, Tweed Forum, *River Till Restoration Strategy*, March 2013 available to view online at:
http://tweedforum.org/projects/current-projects/TRRS_web.pdf, pp. 24, 55

37. Mackenzie, Eneas, Volume I, Second Edition, 1825, pp. 374-5

38. *The Gentleman's Magazine*, Volume XCII, Part The Second, London, 1822, p. 17

39. William Whellan & Co., p. 704

40. Stoddart, Thomas Tod, *The Angler's Companion to The Rivers and Lochs of*

NOTES

Scotland, William Blackwood and Sons, Edinburgh and London, 1847, pp. 336-7

41. *Keys to the Past* ref. N19526

42. ibid. ref. N2010

43. ibid., refs. N2034, N2046

44. ibid., ref. N1942; also, SINE website page:
http://sine.ncl.ac.uk/view_structure_information.asp?struct_id=788

45. English Heritage ID: 238029

46. .*Keys to the Past* ref. N1833

47. ibid., ref. N19684

48. English Heritage ID: 238034

49. Wallis, John, p. 479

50. Dickens, Tony, pp. 43, 52

51. *Keys to the Past* ref. N1884

52. ibid., refs. 24246, N24245, N24244, N24247

53. Hugill, Robert, *Borderland Castles & Peles*, ed. J. Burrow & Co. Ltd., London, 1939, reprinted by Sandhill Press Ltd., Morpeth, 1996, p. 101

54. Mackenzie, Eneas, Volume I, Second Edition, 1825, pp. 368-70

55. *Keys to the Past* ref. N1832

56. ibid., ref. N1813

57. See Northumberland Wildlife Trust information at:
www.nwt.org.uk/reserves/ford-moss

58. See Durham Mining Museum information at: www.nwt.org.uk/reserves/ford-moss; also, SINE Project information at:
http://sine.ncl.ac.uk/view_structure_information.asp?struct_id=1105

59. Northumberland Rock Art Web Access to the Beckensall Archive:
http://rockart.ncl.ac.uk/panel_detail_management.asp?pi=11

60. *Keys to the Past* ref. N1958

61. English Heritage ID: 1006601

~

CHAPTER 7—Ford Bridge to Tweed

1. Hutchinson, W., *A View of Northumberland with an Excursion to The Abbey of Mailross in Scotland*, Vol. II, Newcastle, 1776, pp. 337-8

2. ibid.

3. SINE Project, Structure Details for Ford Forge:
http://sine.ncl.ac.uk/view_structure_information.asp?struct_id=1390

4. Douglas, David, *History of the Baptist Churches in the North of England from 1648 to 1845*, Houlston and Stoneman, London; Finlay and Charlton, Newcastle;

William Innes, Edinburgh, 1846, p. 248

5. ibid., p. 249

6. ibid., p. 294

7. Catherall, G. A., 'The Baptists of North Northumberland', *Baptist Quarterly*, 4 Oct. 1965, pp. 169-173

8. *Keys to the Past* ref. N1879

9. Warren, W. L., *Henry II*, University of California Press, 1977, p. 351, drawing on Raine, *History and Antiquities of North Durham*, appendix, 141, nos 782-3; Van Caenegem, *Royal Writs*, 435, nos 47, 47a

10. Neville, Hastings M., *Under a Border Tower etc.*, Mawson, Swan & Morgan, Newcastle-on-Tyne, Second Edition, 1897, pp. 148-9 (first edition 1896)

11. ibid., pp. 151-2

12. Mawer, Allen, p. 108

13. English Heritage ID: 23803

14. For more information, see http://heatherslawlightrailway.co.uk/

15. Parson, Wm. & White, Wm., p. 507

16. Vickers, Kenneth H., *A History of Northumberland*, Volume XI, Northumberland County History Committee, Newcastle-Upon-Tyne, 1922, pp. 436-40

17. Northumberland Communities website page: http://communities.northumberland.gov.uk/Crookham.htm

18. Parson & White Trade Directory, 1828, see http://communities.northumberland.gov.uk/005003FS.htm

19. Kelly's Trade Directory, 1910, see http://communities.northumberland.gov.uk/004975FS.htm

20. Graham, P. Anderson, *Highways and Byways in Northumbria*, Macmillan and Co., London, 1921, p. 69

21. English Heritage Battlefield Report: Flodden 1513, 1995

22. Vickers, Kenneth H., pp. 9-10

23. Parson, Wm. & White, Wm., p. 508

24. Graham, P. Anderson, pp. 61-2

25. *Keys to the Past* ref. N1870. Also, Vickers, Kenneth H., p. 451

26. ibid., ref. N13500

27. Vickers, Kenneth H., p. 451. Also, Graham, P. Anderson, p. 66

28. Parson, Wm. & White, Wm., p. 508

29. Neville, Hastings M., p. 306

30. English Heritage ID: 238050

31. ibid., ID: 238051

NOTES

32. For more details on the families at Etal, see Parson, Wm. & White, Wm., p. 505; also, Urban, Sylvanus, *The Gentleman's Magazine*, Volume CI, Part the First, January to June, 1831, p. 370

33. Gilly, Rev. Dr., *The Peasantry of the Border. An Appeal in their Behalf "Give them good Cottages, and help them to educate their children"*, pamphlet, 1841. Reproduced in *The Gardener's Magazine*, Vol. XVIII, conducted by J. C. Louden, London, 1842, p. 31

33. English Heritage Listing ID: 238044

34. Northumberland Communities website:
http://communities.northumberland.gov.uk/009598FS.htm

35. English Heritage Listing ID: 238045

36. ibid., ID 238043

37. Graham, P. Anderson, p. 65

38. Dickens, Tony, pp. 47, 49

39. Mawer, Allen, p. 78

40. *Keys to the Past* ref. N1809; Neville, Hastings M., p. 306

41. *Keys to the Past* ref. N2371

42. Neville, Hastings M., p. 309

43. See www.ford-and-etal.co.uk/what-to-do/fishing

44. Parson, Wm. & White, Wm., p. 513; Durham Mining Museum:
www.dmm.org.uk/colliery/e036.htm

45. English Heritage SAM list entry number: 1006622

46. Parson, Wm. & White, Wm., p. 341

47. Northumberland Communities webpage:
http://communities.northumberland.gov.uk/Duddo.htm

48. English Heritage Listing ID: 238020

49. English Heritage Listing ID: 238019

50. English Heritage Listing ID: 238021

51. SINE Project, Structure Details for Duddo Tower:
http://sine.ncl.ac.uk/view_structure_information.asp?struct_id=87

52. Hugill, Robert, p. 83

53. *Keys to the Past* ref. N2371; Durham Mining Museum:
www.dmm.org.uk/colliery/g004.htm

54. Duddo Community Website: http://www.duddo.org.uk/index.php/about-duddo/

55. Mawer, Allen, pp. 66, 233

56. English Heritage Listing ID: 238024

57. Address by Ralph Carr, President, to *The Berwickshire Naturalists' Club* at

Whittingham, September 13th 1860, p. 179

58. MacFarlane, Robert, *The Old Ways, A Journey on Foot*, Penguin Books, London & elsewhere, 2012, p. 44

59. English Heritage Listing ID: 238001

60. Hutchinson, W., pp. 22-3

61. Leyland, John, *The Itinery in or about the years 1535-1543*, Parts IX, X, AND XI, ed. Lucy Toulmin Smith, G. Bell and Sons, London, 1910, p. 64

62. Wallis, John, p. 458

63. Mackenzie, Eneas, Volume I, Second Edition, 1825, p. 341

64. Mawer, Allen, p. 108

65. *Keys to the Past* ref. N2360

66. See www.mouthofthetweed.co.uk/040%20Milling.pdf

67. Metherell, Chris, *Scarce, Rare & Extinct Vascular Plant Register*, North Northumberland Vice County 68, 2011

68. SINE Project, Structure Details for Twizel Mill: http://sine.ncl.ac.uk/view_structure_information.asp?struct_id=1351

69. Sine Project, Structure Details for Blake's Follyhttp://sine.ncl.ac.uk/view_structure_information.asp?struct_id=1429

70. Mawer, Allen, p. 202

71. English Heritage Listing ID: 1020743

72. See Oxford DNB: www.oxforddnb.com/templates/article.jsp?articleid=73890&back

73. Leyland, John, p. 64

74. English Heritage Listing ID: 1018445

75. Mackenzie, Eneas, Volume I, Second Edition, 1825, p. 336

76. English Heritage description and listing ID: 1018445

77. English Heritage description and listing ID: 1001053

78. National Archives Reference: BRO 129

79. ibid., BRO 129/1/3/12

80. Wallis, John, p. 452

81. See Townsend, C. C., *Parietaria Officinalis and P. Judaica*, at http://archive.bsbi.org.uk/Wats6p365.pdf

82. Gerard, John, *The Herball or General Historie of Plantes*, Lond., 1636, pp. 330-1

83. Walter Scott, *Marmion: A Tale of Flodden Field*, William Smith, London, 1840, Canto The Sixth, XIX, pp. 234-5

84. Geoffrey of Monmouth, *History of the Kings of Britain*, trans., Aaron Thompson, rev., J. A. Giles, In parentheses Publications Medieval Latin Series, Cambridge,

NOTES

Ontario, 1999, Book V, Ch. 6, p. 77

85. English Heritage description and listing ID: 10304148

86. Mackenzie, Eneas, Volume I, Second Edition, 1825, p. 338

87. English Heritage PastScape ID: 1373

88. *History of the Berwickshire Naturalists' Club*, Vol. XXI.—1909, 1910, 1911, pp. 16-18

89. English Heritage Monument No. 1379

90. Bowes, Sir Robert, *A Booke of the State of the Frontiers and Marches betwixt England and Scotland* written at the request of the Lord Marquis Dorsett, the Warden General, 1550 reproduced in Hodgson, John, *A History of Northumberland in three parts*, Part III, Vol. II, Article III, p. 178

91. Mackenzie, Eneas, Volume I, Second Edition, 1825, p. 338

92. Hutchinson, W., p. 23

93. Bede, pp. 223-33 (Bede IV 27-32)

94. ibid.

95. *History of the Berwickshire Naturalists' Club*, Vol. XXI.—1909, 1910, 1911, p. 16

96.See Cheviot Futures website: www.cheviotfutures.co

Further Reading

These books are recommended in addition to the sources in *Notes*.

Geology

1. ed. Scrutton, C., *Northumbrian Rocks and Landscapes: A Field Guide*, Yorkshire Geological Society, Second Edition, 2005

2. Lebour, G. A., *Outlines of the Geology of Northumberland*, M. and M. W. Lambert, Newcastle-upon-Tyne & Henry Sotheran and Co., London, 1878

~

Wildlife

1. Bonney, Stewart, *Wild Northumberland*, Powdene Publicity, 2012

2. Swan, Prof. George A., *Flora of Northumberland*, Natural History Society of Northumbria, 1993

3. Britton, Dave; Day, John, *Where to Watch Birds in Northeast England: Northumberland, Tyne and Wear, Durham*, Second Edition, Bloomsbury Publishing PLC, 2004

4. Miles, Archie, *Silva*, Ebury Press, 1999. (This is a comprehensive book on British trees)

~

Local History

1. Wilson, Sarah, *Reflections: The Breamish Valley and Ingram*, Northern Heritage, 2005

2. Palmer-Cooper, Joy, *Chatton, A Portrait: A Celebration of Life Past and Present in a North Northumberland Village*, ABE, 2003

3. Roberts, Ian; Carlton, Richard; Rushworth, Alan, *Drove Roads of Northumberland*, History Press, 2010

FURTHER READING

4. Beckensall, Stan, *Northumberland Churches: from the Anglo-Saxons to the Reformation*, Amberley Publishing, 2013

~

Archaeology

1. Oswald, Al; Ainsworth, Stewart; Pearson, Trevor, *Hillforts; Prehistoric Strongholds of Northumberland National Park*, English Heritage, 2007

2. Waddington, Clive; Passmore, Dave, *Ancient Northumberland*, English Heritage, Country Store, 2004

3. Passmore, David Glynn, *Managing Archaeological Landscapes in Northumberland: Till Tweed Studies*, Oxbow Books, 2009

4. Passmore, David Glynn; Waddington, Clive, *Archaeology and Environment in Northumberland: Till Tweed Studies*, Oxbow Books, 2012

5. ed. Mazel, Aron D.; ed. Nash, George; ed. Waddington, Clive, *The Prehistoric Rock-art of Britain*, Archaeopress, 2007

6. For a bibliography of Northumberland Rock-art, individual titles being too numerous to mention here, visit: http://rockart.ncl.ac.uk/bibliography.asp

7. Waddington, Clive; Miket, Roger; Edwards, Benjamin; Johnson, Ben, *Neolithic and Early Historic Settlement in North Northumberland*, Oxbow Press, 2009

8. Waddington, Clive, *Maelmin: An Archaeological Guide*, Country Store, 2001

9. Cunliffe, Barry, *Britain Begins*, Oxford University Press, 2012. (This is a comprehensive book on the origins of the British and Irish peoples from the end of the last Ice Age to the eve of the Norman Conquest)

Index

Maps not indexed; people in *italics*.
Illustrations in **bold**

~

INDEX

257

INDEX